The River Cottage

Herb Handbook

# The River Cottage Herb Handbook

*by* Nikki Duffy

*with an introduction by*
Hugh Fearnley-Whittingstall

www.rivercottage.net

BLOOMSBURY
LONDON · BERLIN · NEW YORK · SYDNEY

*In memory of all my grandparents*

First published in Great Britain 2012

Text © 2012 by Nikki Duffy
Photography © 2012 by Mark Diacono,
except p.46 © GAP Photos/FhF Greenmedia

The moral right of the author has been asserted

Bloomsbury Publishing Plc, 50 Bedford Square, London WC1B 3DP
Bloomsbury Publishing, London, Berlin, New York and Sydney

A CIP catalogue record for this book is available from the British Library
ISBN 978 1 4088 0883 2
10 9 8 7 6 5 4 3 2 1

Project editor: Janet Illsley
Design: willwebb.co.uk
Printed and bound in Italy by Graphicom

www.bloomsbury.com/rivercottage

# Contents

Herbs are central to the River Cottage way of cooking and eating. It's high time that a volume on these lovely ingredients was added to our other handbooks, and I'm delighted that Nikki has been the one to write it. She is as passionate as I am about the culinary properties of these wonderful plants. Like me, she is in thrall to their intoxicating scents and their gorgeous flowers, which are frequently at least as useful as their leaves.

Herbs are often real catalysts, both in the garden and the kitchen. They function in an immediate way, getting the juices flowing because they are so instantly enticing and appetite-piquing. But, in a broader sense, herbs can be the plants that make you into a gardener, even a very small-scale one, and the ingredients that turn you into a creative cook. They are so easy to grow and so simple to use that they form an irresistible first step on a road towards self-sufficiency.

That needn't be the end goal, of course; in fact it's really an endless and ever-life-enhancing journey. That journey, away from industrially produced, sterile food towards everything that is local, seasonal and exciting, is what River Cottage is, and has always been, about. And Nikki's book is now a vital part of that road map. It's a wonderfully useful guide that will introduce you to the satisfaction of growing and cooking some of your own food, if you don't already. If you do, you will find much in these pages to inspire you and take you further. There are plenty of classic recipes here, but also bags of new ideas that will have you using your homegrown herbs in ways you may never have considered before. Bay-infused ice cream, white chocolate truffles with basil, and lavender-scented lamb are just a few among a host of tempting aromatic recipes.

What I love about herbs is their easiness, the lack of effort they require from the cook. These ingredients don't ask you for any big commitment beyond the bid to make something even more delicious to eat. Preparation is usually minimal: pulling some leaves off a stem, maybe chopping them, maybe not. Quantities need not be precise. One herb can often be substituted for another. And while I'd be the first to try to persuade you to grow your own, you don't actually have to do so in order to get good, flavoursome specimens (see Nikki's list of the herbs most worth buying from shops on p.13). And yet, while they ask so little of you, herbs will give and give and give in terms of flavour, colour, texture and that indefinable ability they have to just 'make' a dish.

Herbs were among the first things I tackled when setting up my fledgling kitchen garden at the original River Cottage. I knew that these plants would instantly enliven my cooking, long before I could start lifting my own homegrown potatoes or cutting my first spears of asparagus. So I went and bought some pots of bay, rosemary, parsley and chives from a local nursery, planted them, and I was away. They were ready to cut almost immediately and, with a bit of undemanding maintenance work, they continued to provide me with an aromatic harvest right up to the day we moved out. Now, the altogether larger-scale kitchen plot at Park Farm is absolutely bursting with herbs. Nasturtiums shout from every corner, angelica lifts its long, elegant stems by the farmhouse, and there are beds bristling with chives, mint, parsley, rosemary, sage and lovage to satisfy the kitchen's considerable needs.

While it's not essential to grow your own herbs in order to enjoy them, I do think you're missing a bit of a trick if you don't. Most look and taste their absolute best when freshly cut, and their very presence on your windowsill or by the back door will encourage you to use them. You don't need a veg patch, greenhouse or polytunnel; you can grow herbs with no garden at all. Of course, the more space you have, the more possibilities suggest themselves, but a window box, sunny patio or even a doorstep with a few pots on will suffice.

If you think you know your herbs pretty well, then step outside the zone of what is already familiar to you. Treat yourself to a pot of intense Thai basil or a glowing purple-bronze perilla plant and see how you get on. I am certain you will be won over by these delicious aromatic plants. Browse through the pages of this book and see what else tickles your fancy. With Nikki's warm and wise text to guide you, there is very little to stand in the way of an ever-increasing exploration and enjoyment of the herbal world. Immerse yourself in it, breathe in deeply, and savour the sheer joy that it brings.

## Hugh Fearnley-Whittingstall, East Devon, December 2011

Making the Most
of Herbs

Herbs are beautiful, life-enhancing, seductive things. Whether you see them primarily as plants or as ingredients, they are enticing. I find it hard to believe that anyone could look at a lavender bush nodding in the sunshine, or sniff a torn bay leaf and not experience, at the very least, a flicker of pleasure. And herbs can give much more than that: their aromas, their flavours, their colours and shapes can make you feel positively joyful.

I think the appeal of herbs lies, first of all, in the incredibly strong response we tend to have to their scents. Those intense, penetrating aromas send messages directly to the limbic system, the part of our brain that deals with emotion and memory. One thread of scent can cause the mind to retrieve distinct images, but also more fugitive recollections and feelings that can completely alter our mood. A sniff of rosemary or a breath of thyme can awaken powerful associations with comfort, pleasure and satisfaction. Herbs bypass our thinking, analytical minds and go straight to our hungry souls.

You can enjoy herbs simply by being close to them – by having them in your garden, or in a jug on the windowsill. But if you go one step further and actually use them, you hold in your hands the power to tempt and delight other people (and yourself, of course). By doing something as simple as pouring a cup of mint tea or spooning out some fragrant pesto, you can tap into the deep, instinctive rush of good feeling that these plants evoke. What's more, herbs can enhance and define food in a unique way by adding that crucial aromatic element that gets the mouth watering even before you take the first bite. And the wonderful thing is, they deliver on their promise: they taste as good as they smell.

This is primarily a book about cooking with herbs, about the delicious ways they can flavour and perfume the food you serve. I hope it will encourage you to try herbs that you've not eaten before, and to experiment with new ways of using your old favourites. No one need feel unsure about cooking with these plants. They can be the most liberating and confidence-boosting of ingredients. They allow you to innovate and bring individuality to your cooking while, at the same time, anchoring you in sound culinary tradition because they are often responsible for those key flavours that 'make' a dish (the sage in the stuffing, the tarragon in the béarnaise, the bay in the béchamel).

Some herbs are very strong and can be overpowering in large quantities, but it's still hard to completely ruin a meal by adding too much, in the way you could by overdoing the salt or the chilli powder. Herbs invite experimentation, and rarely make you suffer for it.

This is also, however, a book about growing herbs. That's because, even if your focus is in the kitchen, your garden, greenhouse or windowsill can provide you with raw materials that may otherwise be very difficult to get hold of. Winter savory, scented geraniums and bergamot are rarely to be found for sale as cut herbs, but they can all be at your fingertips if you grow your own. You don't need to be any kind of horticultural whiz (I assure you, I'm no Percy Thrower). You don't even need to be a particularly keen gardener. If you do not have the time or inclination to raise plants from seed or prepare a dedicated herb bed, then you can easily source your herbs as young potted plants from specialist suppliers. Then all you need is some basic know-how on the best way to keep them producing their glorious, fragrant leaves.

I have not written about the medicinal properties of herbs. This is not because I don't have a lot of faith in their power to heal, soothe and relieve, but simply because I am no expert in this huge and complex subject.

There are hundreds, probably thousands, of edible plants that we would classify as herbs and of course I haven't included all of them here. Instead I have limited myself to the ones I know taste good, and which are easy to grow in this country. That is still a very big and very delicious mixed bag which, I hope, you are about to dip into and enjoy.

# Buying herbs

It would be wonderful if we all had the time, space and motivation to grow great armfuls of different herbs in our own backyards, but for most of us that's far from realistic. I certainly don't grow all of the herbs I use. At least some of the time, you're likely to be buying herbs from a retailer. I like sourcing herbs from farm shops and farmers' markets as these often offer a wide choice, very fresh generous bunches, and some free information to boot. However, supermarkets are part of my supply chain too.

When you're looking for fresh herbs in a shop, I would think first and foremost about the variety itself. The more robust herbs, such as bay and rosemary, simply withstand packing and travelling better than their tender brethren. Very pungent herbs, like basil and mint, can also be fine from a packet if they are very fresh. Some of the more delicate, subtle herbs, such as chives and chervil, are nearly always disappointing when bought in packets.

As with any fresh produce, it makes sense to buy herbs within their natural season, where possible. In Britain, this is generally April to September, with a real peak in quality in June, July and August. There are plenty of herbs that a home-grower can produce in the autumn and winter, but the commercial herb season is more restricted. With the probable exception of bay, fresh herbs bought in the winter months will almost certainly be imported. In-season herbs, particularly if they are harvested locally, are likely to taste much better and be more pungent than those that have been transported great distances.

Flat-leaf parsley *Petroselinum crispum* var. *neapolitana*

Almost without exception, the more recently a herb has been picked, the better. So look carefully for signs of freshness including a bright colour, plump stems and perfect, unwilted leaves. If the herb is not wrapped in plastic, then smelling it, or crushing one leaf in your fingers to release its oils, will help you ascertain if it's bursting with flavour or not. If possible, find out when the herb was picked; this certainly may be possible at a farmers' market or in a small greengrocer's. If not, be guided by use-by dates.

Here's a list of the fresh herbs I think most worth shopping for, all of which have the potential, at least, to be flavourful and good when bought from a retailer. I nearly always buy packets or cut bunches. Those pots of 'growing' herbs often have the weediest texture and weakest flavour of all.

**Bay** I use this every day, more or less, so I'd always grow it but, if you can't, the fragrance and flavour survive very well when packaged. Dried bay is just about worth buying too – but fresh is better. (See Bay, p.49.)

**Thyme/lemon thyme** These hardy little herbs hang on to their flavour well, so a packet or bundle should stand you in good stead. (See Thyme/lemon thyme, p.147.)

**Rosemary** Another robust herb that travels pretty well. (See Rosemary, p.125.)

**Garlic** Growing your own is satisfying but if, like me, you use it in great quantity, you may struggle to grow enough to meet all your needs. (See Garlic, p.77.)

**Horseradish** Magnificent gnarled roots of horseradish are becoming easier to find in greengrocer's. It's a wonderful ingredient to use fresh and a well-wrapped root keeps for weeks in the fridge. (See Horseradish, p.82.)

**Basil** This is not the easiest of herbs to grow and it is often required in large amounts – a single pesto recipe could use your whole homegrown crop. I've found very fresh, fragrant bought basil to be absolutely fine. (See Basil, p.44.)

**Flat-leaf parsley** As with basil, it can be hard to keep up with the demand for this tender herb. I often buy large bunches and keep them in a jug of water. They rarely go to waste. (See Parsley, p.113.)

**Marjoram/oregano** If harvested at their peak, these are usually still very pungent and flavourful after a sojourn on the shop shelf. (See Marjoram/oregano p.101.)

**Coriander** Worth buying in bunches provided it's very fresh. (See Coriander, p.66.)

# Picking herbs

If you are picking herbs from a garden, you can obviously have total confidence in their freshness. It's also worth knowing that most herbs reach a peak of aromatic flavour just before flowering – often when buds are forming, but not yet opening. This is the point in the plant's life cycle when it is generally at its strongest and its concentration of essential oils tends to be greatest. If you allow herbs to reach this state then cut them, and keep doing so, you will hold off the actual flowering and hopefully maximise your harvest of flavourful leaves.

Don't stop all your herbs from flowering altogether, though – often the flowers themselves make delicious and beautiful ingredients, and if you want a plant to set seed, it obviously needs to flower first.

# Storing herbs

Once you have fresh herbs back in the kitchen, it pays to use them as soon as possible. However, if you don't need to use them straight away, or you have half a bunch left over, you can prolong their lives a little. I treat them like cut flowers and place them in jugs of water.

First trim the stem ends because these may have dried and formed a seal, rendering them unable to take up fresh water. Put the bunch of herbs into a jug of cool water and keep it away from direct sunlight or the heat from your oven or radiators. Check the herb regularly and change the water as soon as it starts to look murky or smell musty.

In hot, dry weather or, conversely, in the depths of winter when your kitchen may actually be rather warm, it's best to keep fresh herbs in the fridge, in an open plastic bag. This protects them while still allowing ethylene gas, released by the cut stalks, to escape (ethylene hastens decay).

If you are planning to store herbs in the fridge, make sure the leaves are dry, to inhibit rotting. Before putting the herbs in the bag, you can wrap them loosely in a piece of kitchen paper to absorb any vestiges of moisture. Woody herbs such as rosemary, bay and thyme can keep quite well like this for a week or so. For tender parsley, coriander, fennel and the like, you've only got a few days. Basil does not respond well to chilling, so keep it in a cool part of the kitchen rather than in the fridge.

Some herbs, such as chives, may look all right after a few days in the fridge, but their flavour will have all but disappeared.

With a couple of exceptions, discussed later on, I don't buy dried herbs. They just don't cut it in terms of flavour and have a very short shelf life.

Oregano *Origanum vulgare*

# Drying and freezing herbs

There is something appealing about having dried herbs in your kitchen – a bunch or two of thyme hanging from the ceiling, perhaps, or some crumbled sage in a tiny jar – but in most cases there is little point in drying herbs in my view. Delicate grassy, feathery varieties, such as chervil, parsley, chives or coriander, cannot be dried successfully. It is very hard to capture and retain the inimitable scents and flavours they deliver when fresh, because the compounds that provide these evaporate along with the water from their leaves. With woodier herbs, such as thyme, rosemary, savory, myrtle, bay, lavender, and also with mint, marjoram and lovage, you will still get flavour from the dried leaves or flowers. In fact, it can be very concentrated. But it is never, to my taste, as good, clear, sweet and true as the flavour of the fresh herb.

As always, there are some exceptions. It's worth drying some fennel seeds for winter roasts, for instance, and maybe some lavender flowers for Christmas biscuits and cakes. If you are inclined to drying herbs, remember that the more delicate the flavour and texture of the herb, the less likely it is to dry successfully.

Gather herbs for drying when their flavour is at its peak, usually just before flowering. They must be completely dry – mid-morning on a warm, sunny day is a good time. Lay them on a rack and place in an airing cupboard or very low oven (maximum 30°C) with the door slightly open. Never try to dry them in the sun.

The drying process may take a few hours or a few days, depending on the variety and the conditions. Stop when the herbs are dry and brittle, but still green and fragrant. Try putting a sprig of the dried herb into a jam jar, closing the lid and leaving it for a few hours. If any moisture or condensation appears, the herb is not 'done'. Once dried, strip the leaves from the stems and transfer them to perfectly dry glass jars, preferably dark-coloured. Seal, label and store in a cool, dry, dark place. Use within a year.

Freezing is also reasonably successful in some cases, especially with those tender herbs that don't dry well at all, such as basil and parsley. Pick perfect, undamaged leaves, divide into the sort of quantities you think you'll be using, and wrap loosely but securely in foil or cling film before freezing. Once defrosted, you can add them to dishes as you would fresh herbs. The flavour should still be good but their texture and colour will have been altered. They'll have darkened and become limp, so they won't be much use for garnishing or salads.

Another way of freezing herbs is in ice. Chop the herb and pack into ice-cube trays, pouring over a little water before freezing them into solid herb blocks.

There are other methods of preserving herbal flavours which I do think are very worthwhile – namely herb butters and purées, such as pesto, which freeze well, and flavoured vinegars and jellies. You'll find recipes for these later in the book.

# Flavour chemistry

I go into detail on methods of cooking individual herbs in the main body of this book. However, there are some basics which are worth understanding at the outset.

Herbs are imbued with various compounds which give flavour and aroma. The general idea, when cooking, is to release those compounds from the plant so you can smell and taste them while you're eating. Some herbal flavours are released so readily that it's best to simply eat the herb fresh, whole and raw so the flavours are set free in your mouth. As soon as you start chopping and heating and exposing to air, that fugitive flavour is lost. Other compounds are a little less ethereal and can be captured and held in a dish.

The various traditional ways of using herbs that have evolved over the centuries reflect accumulated knowledge on how best to control those all-important compounds. And every time you cook with herbs you, too, are making choices about how to manipulate those essential chemicals, even if you don't realise you're doing so.

It is often the more woody-stemmed herbs with their relatively robust leaves that have the most stable, long-lived flavour compounds. In many cases, these are plants which are natives of hot places – they have evolved to conserve water and they tend to retain their flavour with it. Imagine wild thyme or rosemary baking under a Mediterranean sun and you'll get a feeling for the way the flavour is held fast in their leaves, concentrated, pungent and penetrating.

With delicate thin-leaved herbs, the flavour compounds are usually more volatile and evaporate easily, which is why some herbs such as chives and basil almost completely lose their flavour when cooked.

There are also in-between herbs – parsley, lovage and fennel spring to mind – which can take a bit of heat. Their flavour may well change during light cooking, but they will still inform the dish. And often you can get very delicious results by adding the same herb both at the beginning and the end of cooking, creating a multi-layered experience of its flavour.

It's not just heat that helps to liberate flavour, damage to the plant's cell membranes has a similar effect. Whole sprigs or bouquets garnis added to slow-cooked dishes, with perhaps just a twist or a light whack with a rolling pin to help release the flavour, will have a relatively subtle, mellow influence. The same herbs, finely chopped, will give a much more pungent effect.

It's also worth knowing that these flavour compounds are usually more soluble in fat than in water and so can be drawn out by immersion in various plant oils and animal fats. If you stir rosemary into an oily dressing, or beat chopped parsley into butter, there will be a release of flavour. If you put sprigs of the same herbs in a jug of cold water, without first bruising or chopping them, not much would happen.

# Chopping

To chop herbs finely, strip the leaves from the stems and place them on a large chopping board. It's much easier to chop herbs well if they are dry so, after washing, give them a whiz in a salad spinner or pat dry carefully with a clean tea towel.

Choose a large, reasonably heavy, sharp cook's knife. Holding the handle firmly in one hand, place the fingers of your other hand on top of the blade, at the pointed end. Use your fingers to anchor this end of the knife on the board, then work the handle end up and down, across the herb leaves, gradually reducing them to a finely chopped state. You'll need to stop and change direction a few times and perhaps scoop and redistribute the herbs on the board to achieve a nice even chop.

# Shredding

Herbs with fairly large, thin leaves, such as mint or basil, can be very good when finely shredded. The technical term for these ribboned herbs is a 'chiffonade'. Stack several leaves on top of one another then roll them up tightly into a 'cigar'. Secure the cigar with one hand, keeping your fingers tucked in, then slice very thinly with a large, sharp knife.

# Tying a bouquet garni

A bouquet garni is simply a bundle of herbs used to infuse flavour into soups, stews and stocks. There are no hard and fast rules as to what to include, except that bay is pretty much essential. I would always include thyme, too, and either a strip of leek or a length of celery stalk, plus a handful of parsley stalks. These are the classic fail-safe bouquet garni herbs, but you might like to branch out a bit with sprigs of rosemary or marjoram. Sage, winter savory and lovage can be used too, and these will contribute more distinctive flavours.

Keep the herbs you want to use in large sprigs. Cut a piece of cotton string and lay it on a board, then place the bundle of herbs on top. Bring the ends of the string up over the herbs and tie them tightly.

Alternatively, you can use a small piece of fine muslin to enclose the herbs. Lay the muslin over a tea cup, so it sinks to form a little bag. Put the herbs in the middle, bring the edges of the muslin up around them and secure with cotton string. This is an effective method if you want to include peppercorns or a whole garlic clove in your bouquet. It's also good with rosemary, which often tends to shed its leaves when cooked for a long time.

# Preparing garlic

A garlic clove, with its paper-thin skin tightly hugging the crisp, juicy, pungent inner flesh, is a ticket to all sorts of delicious destinations. It is, therefore, well worth mastering a few simple techniques that will enable you to liberate its amazing flavour without faffing and frustration. You'll find more about this unbelievably versatile and delicious ingredient on pp.77–81.

Peeling This is one of those slightly fiddly jobs that can become irksome if you have to do it over and over. My preferred way is to put the garlic clove on a board then press down on it, slowly and firmly, with the flat blade of a large knife, just until I hear a little crack. This is the skin releasing its hold. Slice off the flat end of the clove and the skin should then be easy to remove.

Crushing There are various ways of doing this, just use whichever you find easiest. Garlic snobs eschew the proprietary garlic crusher; I'm not entirely sure why, although I do think they can be tricky to clean. I prefer to simply crush garlic on a board, with the flat of a knife.

Put a little pinch of salt on your board first, to help your knife get to grips with the garlic, and to draw out its juices. Put the peeled garlic clove on top and then the flat of the knife blade. Smash the clove to break it open then scrape the blade over it again and again until you have a sticky garlic purée.

A pestle and mortar is another useful tool for crushing garlic – again, much easier with a pinch of salt.

If you don't fancy crushing, then grating garlic on a fine grater is an easy way to achieve very similar results.

Chopping The easiest way to get a nice finely chopped bit of garlic is to apply a classic onion-chopping technique. Hold the clove on a board and slice it fairly thinly, but leave it intact at the root end. Turn the clove on its side and slice again, perpendicular to the first cuts, but still keeping it uncut at the far end. Then slice across the clove, so you're cutting fine dice. This gives you a medium-fine chop.

For a really fine or minced finish, use the basic chopping technique for leafy herbs (see p.18), working your knife backwards and forwards over the chopped garlic to reduce it to smaller and smaller pieces.

Crushing garlic

Chopping garlic

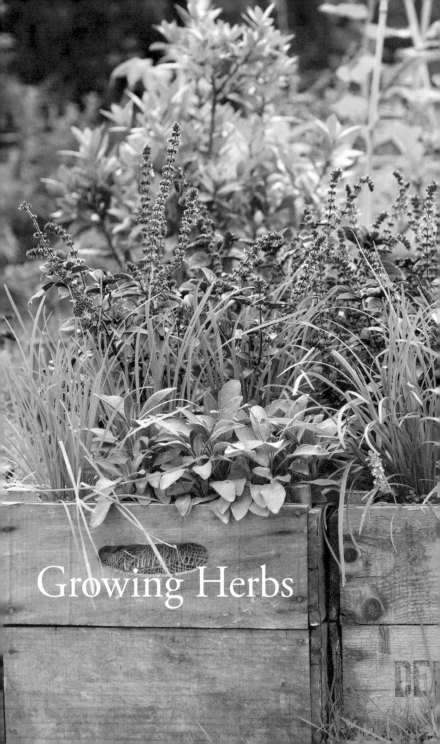

Growing Herbs

If you enjoy cooking with herbs and particularly if you want to expand your repertoire beyond the fabulous but familiar five – parsley, thyme, rosemary, sage and bay – I would wholeheartedly encourage you to grow some. Of course, it helps if you have a garden, or at least an outside space that will accommodate a few pots, but it is by no means essential.

## Why grow herbs?

Quite simply, so that you can eat them. You can buy a reasonable range of the more commonly used herbs from retailers, but you will never get a true experience of the extraordinary range of scents, savours and textures that herbs can provide if you don't grow some of them yourself. A cook can get by with packets of parsley, coriander and thyme from the shops, but with some shrubby lemon verbena and hyssop, a glorious angelica plant and a few pots of savory, celery leaf and bergamot growing outside the back door, your culinary opportunities are vastly increased.

The freshness of homegrown herbs is always a boon. Quantity is another advantage. If you want to make mint tea every day, or a batch of chervil soup or sorrel sauce, then you need big handfuls of fresh herbs, which can be expensive to buy. The converse is also true: herbs such as lovage and sage are often best used in small quantities – buy even a diminutive bunch and you may well find a lot of it going to waste.

One final reason for growing these edible plants is their sheer beauty. Even if you never eat a single leaf, herbs will enhance any plot. Group a few together, whether in pots or your own little herb patch, and you'll be rewarded by a panoply of shades of green, a variety of forms, and many different and glorious flowers. You will bring bees and butterflies to your garden, and probably ward off unwanted insects too. And you will have the opportunity to crush a few aromatic leaves between your fingers whenever you feel like it, just for the sheer joy of their scent.

## Preparing to grow

If you were to make a careful plan of the perfect garden for growing a big range of herbs, you'd need full sun, partial shade, dappled shade, sheltered spots, open spaces, rich soil, sandy soil, chalky soil, moist soil, poor soil, a big range of pots and a greenhouse. Well, I have only a few of these conditions in my garden, and I've still managed to grow nearly all the herbs in this book, so don't feel limited by the garden you've got. Most soils can be improved, most conditions can be created or mimicked, and a great many herbs can be grown in pots, which gives you the ability to change their environment easily. And, at the end of the day, most herbs are pretty forgiving. I constantly remind myself of an adage in *The River Cottage Cookbook*: 'The plants you put out really want to grow. You don't have to make them, you just have to let them.' That's as true with herbs as any other edible plant.

In addition, a herb can reward you so easily and so readily because in the vast majority of cases you're not waiting for it to fruit or produce a sizeable root, seed or other edible appendage. At the minimum, all you need is a few leaves, perhaps a flower or two. And with a bit of preparation and some simple maintenance, most herb plants will give you far more than that.

## Sunlight

Once you've decided what you'd like to grow (see Herb A–Z, pp.38–155), the first thing to establish is whether your herb likes sun or shade. Once it is planted, the amount of sunlight it gets is the thing you have least control over. Most gardens have spots that receive plenty of sun, and others that are dappled or shady. The majority of the herbs in this book enjoy bright conditions, but some will thrive in shady conditions too.

Top five herbs to grow in shady places

| | |
|---|---|
| Angelica | see p.40 |
| Bergamot | see p.53 |
| Sorrel | see p.138 |
| Sweet cicely | see p.142 |
| Wild garlic | see p.153 |

## Soil type and drainage

Once you know which area to put your herb in, you can think about preparing the soil. You need to understand what kind of soil you've got. This is something you can do by digging up a few forkfuls, working it over in your hands, and having a good look at it. It might be light, dry and sandy; it might be heavy, wet, dense and clay-like; or it may be a lovely crumbly dark loam. The latter is particularly desirable, but any soil type can be worked with.

A 'rich' or 'good' soil is one that is full of decomposing organic matter and therefore nutrients. A lot of plants like such a soil, which is why, generally speaking, digging in some good well-rotted compost before planting – and then applying more from time to time as a 'mulch' (a layer on top) – will boost the growth of whatever you plant. For some herbs, a really rich soil is ideal and added nutrients in the form of well-rotted manure are helpful. However, others prefer what is termed a 'poor' soil, which is not very rich in nutrients at all. In this case, go easy on the compost, but don't leave it out altogether.

You will see that I suggest growing almost every herb in this book in well-drained soil. There may be some which like moist or damp conditions, but still drainage is important. I don't know of any herb that likes sitting in waterlogged earth, and wet conditions can lead to failure to thrive and all sorts of rotting and fungal problems, as well as outright death of the plant. So ensuring good drainage is one of the best preparatory steps you can take, whether you're looking at an expansive herb bed or a few little pots. You may be lucky enough to have a garden of lovely friable, lightly sandy loam already, i.e. the kind of soil that drains well naturally. If not, then adjusting drainage qualities is a straightforward though sometimes physically demanding task.

If you dig good well-rotted compost into your soil before planting, you will open up its structure as well as enriching it. The latest horticultural thinking tends to go against frequent digging in, which can potentially disturb a healthy soil ecology and certainly releases carbon. And, obviously, you can't do much digging in if you already have established plants growing. But it's still something worth doing initially, to prepare a plot or a specific small area, especially if you need to improve soil condition and drainage.

In a very dry sandy soil, compost will actually enhance the moisture-holding properties as well as adding nutrients, and you can boost the richness further with manure. In a heavy soil, compost will aid drainage. A soil that is naturally heavy and claggy will benefit further from the addition of sharp sand, of the kind you can buy from any DIY outlet. If you have a really dense clay-based soil, then some sand is pretty much essential. You might want to go one step further and add grit, which is also available from garden centres. Grit is almost always a good idea for herbs such as lavender and rosemary, which prefer dry conditions and a very free-draining soil.

Even with some preparation and improvement, it still makes sense to work with rather than against the soil you've got. If you have light, sandy, poor soil, then you are on to a winner with Mediterranean herbs such as thyme and rosemary. If you have a rich, moisture-retaining soil and shady patches, you should have no trouble with angelica and bergamot. But no herb is beyond your reach: garden soil itself is one thing, what you put in a pot is quite another.

Another factor is the pH value of your soil, which affects the availability of different nutrients. You can check this easily with an inexpensive tester kit from your local garden centre. Most herbs like a fairly neutral soil with a pH between 6.5 and 7 but don't panic unless your soil departs wildly from that in either direction. If it does, there are steps you can take: agricultural lime will raise the pH of a very acid soil, and good compost will help to correct a very alkaline one.

## Container growing

If the soil you have seems hopelessly inappropriate for something you want to grow, or you've run out of soil space in a sunny corner, turn to container gardening, which gives you much more control. Even big, fast-growing perennial herbs such as mint can thrive in a container – if it's large and deep enough and you keep the plant watered and fed. Pots are great, of course, but consider half-barrels, old baths or sinks, buckets, fruit crates, even polystyrene boxes.

If you are planting herbs in pots or containers, drainage is still very important. Preparatory potting composts are designed to be free draining. If you are mixing your own, including some sand in the mix is helpful. And before you put anything into a pot at all, make sure it has a hole at the bottom for drainage. Standard plant pots will already have one but if you are improvising with containers such as welly boots, old buckets or crates, you must make a few small holes in the base.

Before you fill any pot or container with earth or compost, line the base with a shallow layer of 'crocks'. These are conventionally bits of broken pot but could be pebbles or small stones or even chunks of broken-up polystyrene – from a plant tray, perhaps. The idea is to provide a free-draining layer so the soil in the pot will never become waterlogged. All this free drainage does mean, of course, that you need to water pots regularly, especially in warm weather, to keep that moisture passing through.

If you have little or no garden space, there are lots of herbs which grow well in relatively small pots indoors or on a windowsill. Those which don't include plants which are naturally tall or large in stature, such as lovage, bergamot or fennel, and those with long, thick roots, such as angelica and horseradish.

### Top choices for windowsill-growing

| | |
|---|---|
| Basil (any variety) | see p.44 |
| Chives | see p.63 |
| Coriander | see p.66 |
| Lemongrass | see p.94 |
| Marigold | see p.98 |
| Marjoram and oregano | see p.101 |
| Nasturtium | see p.110 |
| Parsley | see p.113 |
| Rosemary | see p.125 |
| Scented geranium | see p.135 |
| Summer savory | see p.141 |

# Compost

It is easy to make your own compost and a great way to recycle household waste if you have a garden with space for a compost bin. If you are looking to improve your soil right here, right now and you have no homemade compost to hand, then you can buy an organic soil improver (see Directory, p.249), which will do a similar job.

**Making your own compost** You will need a compost bin or a bespoke composting container of some kind to contain the compost, keep away unwelcome animals and allow you to mix and aerate the contents easily. This should be put on bare earth or grass to give worms and soil-borne bacteria easy access, as they help break down compost. A reasonably sunny site is ideal because warmth speeds decomposition.

Feed your bin with raw fruit, vegetable and herb trimmings, crushed eggshells, used tea bags and coffee grounds, grass clippings, prunings, young annual weeds that haven't formed seeds, dead leaves and torn-up newspaper or cardboard. To get the right chemical balance and texture, keep an even mix of wetter, quicker-to-decompose 'green' waste (grass and vegetable matter) and drier, tougher 'brown' waste (woody garden trimmings, egg shells, paper and cardboard). Compost needs air, so mix it from time to time with a garden fork, and don't compact it.

Once your bin is full, you need to leave the compost alone to give it time to break down into a crumbly dark brown mass, which can take up to a year. So, ideally you need two bins on the go: one that's full and rotting down, one that you're feeding.

For more information on home-composting, I recommend the *River Cottage Veg Patch Handbook*, as well as www.recyclenow.com/home_composting.

**Potting composts** If you are planting herbs in pots, you'll need to fill them with a 'growing medium'. You can simply scoop up earth from your garden, but it will come with its own cargo of weed seeds. The alternative is to use a potting compost.

Many proprietary potting composts contain extracted peat, which is an environmental no-no and goes against the principles of organic gardening, although there are some organic potting composts which use 'derived' peat, filtered from water that's run naturally from peat moors. However, it's easy to buy peat-free potting composts specifically designed for growing vegetables and herbs.

The other alternative is to mix up your own potting compost using fine, weed-free garden topsoil (mole hills are good, apparently), along with homemade compost that has rotted down to a fine, crumbly consistency, plus some sand and a moisture-retaining material such as vermiculite, perlite or composted bark. The relative amounts of each vary: there are many different recipes to be found. This is probably a project for devoted large-scale gardeners who have plenty of good topsoil to spare and a well-established composting system. Homemade potting compost will not be sterile and completely weed free, as a bought compost will.

# Growing from seed

Growing herbs from seed is immensely satisfying and gives you a lot of control over what you're growing and how it is treated. You can buy almost any herb you might want to grow as a seed, if you look to specialist suppliers (see Directory, p.248), and you will invariably have seedlings aplenty to give away to your friends. However, seed-raising involves more work, more space and more care than simply buying young plants. In addition, some herbs are difficult to raise from seed and some varieties will not 'come true' if started in this way, which means new plants won't be exactly the same as their parents.

Unless you have a potting shed and plenty of time to devote to cosseting your seedlings, you might find it best to buy most of your herbs as young plants, growing just a select few from seed. I go for more unusual herbs as well as annuals that need to be raised afresh every year. Growing from seed is also more economical and effective with annual herbs which you might want to use in large quantities and/or those which run to seed fairly quickly. These can be sown successionally, every few weeks in the spring and summer, so you always have a good crop coming through.

## Top herbs to grow from seed

| Basil | see p.44 |
|-------|----------|
| Chervil | see p.60 |
| Coriander | see p.66 |
| Nasturtiums | see p.110 |
| Perilla | see p.117 |
| Summer savory | see p.141 |
| Thai basil | see p.47 |

Growing most herbs from seed is pretty straightforward and I have given suggestions for the optimum techniques in each A–Z entry. But I am also wedded to the basic River Cottage principle of 'seed packet gardening', i.e. do what it says on the pack and you can't go far wrong.

## When to sow

As a general rule, herb seeds should be sown in spring. There are a few exceptions: angelica and sweet cicely both need to be sown in autumn, for instance, because they will not germinate without a spell of cold weather. And there are others, such as parsley and rocket, that you can sow at pretty much any time of year. But spring is optimum in most cases.

## Where to sow

Some seeds need a lot of warmth to germinate and should be sown indoors or in a greenhouse. Some must be sown outdoors due to temperature requirements, such as angelica and sweet cicely (see When to sow, left). Others, such as dill and coriander, need to go directly into their growing site – be it ground or container – because they don't like being disturbed and replanted. But many can be sown indoors or out. Generally, in early spring when the ground is still cold, say late February to early April, inside is good. As the year progresses, the ground warms and the days lengthen, outside sowing becomes feasible.

Observe when the weeds are starting to sprout in your garden and this will give you a clue as to when it's worth sowing outside. To quote gardening writer Sarah Raven: 'If nature's doing it, you do it too.' Dig, bash and rake the soil to as fine a consistency as possible, removing all weeds as you go. Water it before sowing so the seeds go into a moist environment.

## Equipment

For indoor or greenhouse sowing, invest in plug trays, or module trays. These make it very easy to remove a seedling and move it to a pot or growing site. Open seed trays are less easy to use and you're more likely to damage your seedlings when removing them. Guttering is another good seed receptacle, see p.33.

Fill your plugs with a good seed compost. Special seed composts are fine-textured and have fewer nutrients in them than potting composts. This is because, initially, the germinating seed contains all the nutrients it needs within its case. Added extras aren't necessary; indeed some can actually damage the seed, and they'll also give an unwelcome boost to other competitive weeds or organisms. Some seed packets call for a 'soil-less' seed compost. This often means a peat-based compost, which isn't a good idea (see p.29). However, you can buy peat-free seed composts (see Directory, p.249).

## Sowing herb seeds

Most seeds like darkness to germinate, i.e. they need to be covered with compost or soil, not lying on top of it. A light covering is usually enough. However, as soon as the shoots have started to appear, they need plenty of light so, if they're not already outdoors, they should be in a greenhouse or on a windowsill.

Most seeds need moisture to germinate but they should definitely not be kept wet. Give them a light sprinkling of water after the initial sowing – or spritz with a plant spray bottle. With very fine seeds in plugs, it's better to sit the plug trays in a tray of water so the compost can absorb moisture from the base up. Lift out the plug trays when the compost is moist. In all cases, keep a close eye on your seedlings and give just enough light watering to keep the compost moist.

Coriander seedlings growing in guttering

## Transplanting or thinning out your seedlings

After germination, herb plants will first produce a pair of baby leaves which look similar on most plants. After that, 'true' leaves will form, which look like the ones you'll be harvesting. Once a seedling has several true leaves and looks robust, if it's in a plug, it's time to transplant it – roots need room to grow and seed compost will no longer provide enough nutrients. Transplant healthy-looking seedlings into pots filled with potting compost. Once these have developed into strong young plants, they can be moved again – either into larger containers, or into the garden itself.

If you are sowing seeds directly in the garden, you will need to 'thin out' the baby seedlings. This means removing some of the plants to leave the strongest ones growing with plenty of space around them. The space you should leave varies from plant to plant, so refer to the seed packet. If you don't thin out, individual plants will struggle to get enough light, air and nutrients from the soil.

Seedlings that have been started indoors will benefit from a period of 'hardening off' before being moved outside. This simply means breaking them in gently to outside temperatures and conditions by putting them outside in the day, then bringing them in at night. A week of this should be plenty for most herbs.

## Protecting your seedlings

Seedlings outdoors will need protection from marauding gastropods, birds, rabbits and so on. For slugs and snails, try broken egg shells, beer traps, copper rings, plant collars or any other method of control available from organic gardening suppliers. A cover of fine horticultural mesh is a good barrier against larger predators, as well as many flying pests. Cloches or frames can be used to protect individual plants – you can get some very nifty self-supporting pop-up mesh 'tents' now too.

## Seeds in guttering

Growing seeds in lengths of guttering is a clever technique, used by River Cottage head gardener Mark Diacono. When ready to transplant, you can simply ease the entire length of compost out of the end of the guttering into some prepared ground.

Guttering can also provide you with a harvest of tasty 'micro-leaves', which can be cut as little as 10 days after sowing – to scatter in salads or on soups. Herbs with quite delicate, fast-growing aromatic leaves, such as basil, coriander and chervil, are ideal. Fill a length of guttering – whatever you have room for – with seed compost. You can leave the ends open, letting the compost shelve off gently, or you can seal off the ends with gaffer tape. Sow the seeds fairly thickly down the middle and cover with another thin layer of compost. Water only very lightly – just enough to keep the compost moist – and keep in a warm, light place such as a greenhouse or on a windowsill. Your seeds should begin sprouting within a few days and micro-leaves will be ready to harvest in a couple of weeks, if not sooner.

# Taking cuttings of perennial herbs

This is a good way to propagate woodier herbs, including rosemary and lavender, which do not always grow true and easy from seed. In the spring or early summer when the plant is sending out vigorous new growth, carefully pull away strong new offshoots of non-flowering stem. They should have a small 'heel', or strip of the main stem, still attached at the base. Remove the lower leaves and plant immediately in potting compost with extra sand mixed in. Cover the cutting loosely with a plastic bag, with a couple of little holes snipped in it, to create a humid environment. Put somewhere warm but out of bright sunlight. Keep the compost moist. Remove the bag after a few weeks. Let the plant develop plenty of roots before planting it in the garden or a larger pot during the following spring or summer.

**Propagating rosemary cuttings**

# Buying plants

Shopping for herb plants is a delicious and exciting pastime. In a decent nursery, or even browsing the pages of an internet supplier, you can easily get carried away, purchasing more than you had initially intended. The beauty of buying herbs as young plants is that all the crucial work of germination and early nurturing has been done for you. With many plants, you can start harvesting straight away. They will at the very least be established and ready to plant in a larger pot, or the garden.

There are only two cons, as far as I can see. Firstly, it costs more to buy a couple of plants than a packet of seeds which could, potentially, give you tens of specimens. Secondly, you don't know how that herb has been nurtured and raised. A herb may have been treated with artificial fertilisers, chemical sprays and growth hormones which are absorbed into the leaves. I prefer to buy herb plants from specialist herb suppliers. Some are certified organic and even those who aren't will often be very willing to talk to you about how their plants are treated and raised. If you've bought perennial herbs from a source you're not sure about, you can plant them and wait for a year before using them, until a fresh cycle of growth has started. There should be little or no residue in the leaves by then.

# Watering

All plants need water to thrive but the amount they need varies a great deal and very few plants respond well to over-watering. Large perennial herbs, once established in a particular spot, often need no more than rainfall. This is especially true of the Mediterranean herbs, such as lavender, thyme, rosemary and hyssop, which thrive in dry conditions. There are others, however – angelica springs to mind – which really like quite a moist soil all the time. And of course very dry weather can make even well-established plants suffer, so always keep a careful eye on them for signs of wilting and general failure to thrive.

Annual herbs, which will not have the time or inclination to put down such long, deep roots, need more attention, and any herb grown in a pot or container will need watering. As a general rule, keep the soil of pot herbs just damp. Water in the cooler parts of the day – early morning or evening – to minimise evaporation. Be aware, however, that basil is a herb that does not like to 'go to bed wet'.

It is generally better to use rainwater, collected in a water butt and applied with a watering can, than tap water from a hosepipe. Not only is collecting rainwater a good way of conserving this precious resource, but it will also be free of substances such as chlorine, which are routinely added to tap water. Artificially softened tap water is not good for plants as it contains a lot of salt.

# Feeds and fertilisers

It is a central tenet of organic gardening, indeed of most traditional common-sense gardening, that the soil itself gives us everything we need, just as long as we look after it properly. So if you care for your soil, adding organic compost and perhaps manure regularly, you shouldn't need to worry about feeds and fertilisers. These only tend to feed the plant, rather than the soil itself, and they don't do anything to improve soil structure, which compost does. Feeds and fertilisers are also often designed to help a plant produce more fruit, which is not usually relevant for herbs.

However, most successful gardeners would agree that a bit of a boost every now and then can work wonders for some plants, and feeding is important for herbs grown in pots, where there is a much more limited supply of nutrients. Apply liquid feeds perhaps a few times during the growing season, particularly after cutting back. Always err on the side of under- rather than over-feeding. Herbs do not require feeding as much as vegetables or fruit do.

**Organic chicken manure pellets** A few of these can be added to pots early in the season and will slowly release nutrients, which means you don't have to remind yourself about applying fresh feed.

**Organic liquid feeds** I tend to use these as they're so easy to apply. They may be based on seaweed, fungi or on worm casts. If you have your own little wormery (see wigglywigglers.com), it will produce a rich and nutritious wormy liquid that makes an excellent feed.

**Homemade comfrey or nettle 'teas'** These are packed full of nutrients and can really give plants a boost. You can make them by simply soaking a good quantity of comfrey or nettle leaves in a tub full of rainwater for 3–5 weeks. The resulting brew (which will be really quite extraordinarily stinky) can then be diluted and used as a liquid feed.

# Weeds

I know this might sound blooming obvious, but it's certainly something I need to remind myself of often enough: do try and keep your herb patch fairly weed free. One can get a bit blasé about weeds, but remember they are strong, hungry and competitive plants that will take some of the water, nutrients, light and space that you want to go to your beloved herbs.

# My favourite herbs to grow

Any herb that you really enjoy eating is a good one for you to grow, but if you're not quite sure where to begin, these are the ones that I believe best reward the small-scale culinary gardener. I've given my reasons for loving each of them, but all are easy to maintain, beautiful to look at and extremely versatile in the kitchen.

**My top ten herbs to grow at home**

| Bay | p.49 | It is the most useful and versatile herb of all time. |
| Lovage | p.96 | You rarely need more than a few leaves at a time – much easier to pick from your own plant. |
| Rosemary | p.125 | It's always there, winter or summer, and it's an essential herb for roasts. It's also very beautiful and attracts the bees and the butterflies. |
| Lavender | p.86 | It's an underrated culinary herb – and another favourite with the pollinating insects. |
| Mint | p.105 | A cup of freshly brewed real mint tea is the most refreshing thing imaginable. Mint is also endlessly useful and versatile. |
| Chives | p.63 | A fresh-cut chive is a thing of wonder – and a chive flower possibly even better – while one from a packet is emphatically not. A quintessential summer herb. |
| Tarragon | p.144 | It just has the most incredible anise flavour that enhances so many foods. |
| Lemon verbena | p.92 | It is so very pretty and so incredibly fragrant, a wonderful herb for sweets and puds. |
| Angelica | p.40 | You certainly can't buy it fresh, and it's a magnificent plant. It is wonderful cooked with fruit. |
| Borage | p.54 | It is so beautiful and the flowers are incredibly versatile for decorating all sorts of dishes and drinks. |

Herb A–Z

# Angelica *Angelica archangelica*

| PLANT GROUP | Hardy biennial |
| --- | --- |
| HARVEST | May–September |

In its full glory, this is a lovely, generous plant with thick ridged stems, effulgent leaves and bouncing flowerheads. I would grow it for its looks alone, but it's a useful herb too. Angelica has some notes similar to juniper and, like that spice, is one of the classic flavourings for gin. If you're partial to the occasional refreshing 'G and T', you'll probably recognise angelica's astringent, slightly musky but fragrant flavour. There's also a sort of sherbety brightness to it, a tingle on the tongue, which makes it a winning companion to fruit.

## In the kitchen

You can eat very tender young angelica leaves in salads (though I'd attach provisos to this, see below). It's also said that you can cook them lightly, like spinach, while the stems can be steamed like asparagus. I've tried these things and found the results unedifying – even quite young stems and leaves can be bitter and tough. However, angelica really shines when it is cooked with fruit and/or sugar. When you combine it with a tart fruit, such as rhubarb or gooseberries, something wonderful happens. The herb has an acidity-reducing, lightening effect on the flavour of the fruit, which means you can go a little easier on the sugar, and it contributes its own musky flavour too. I always find the stems more effective and flavourful than the leaves – but you can use a mix of the two. Candying angelica is also very definitely worth doing.

- Finely chopped angelica stems can be added to the fruit when making rhubarb, currant or gooseberry jam.
- The very first tender leaves of the year can be used in salads. However, they do have a distinct bitterness, so I would shred them finely and combine them with other herb leaves – try sorrel (p.138) and/or anise hyssop (p.43), as well as some more bland, sweet lettuce-type leaves.
- **Rhubarb crumble with angelica** (p.223)
- **Candied angelica**, plus angelica syrup (p.237)

## How to grow

Because the seeds need to be sown fresh – within a few weeks of coming off the stem – it's a good idea to buy your first angelica as a little fledgling plant. (You can buy the seeds, but they will be dormant and need 'stratifying', which means subjecting to a period of artificial cold weather. This can be done by layering the seeds in damp kitchen paper and putting them in the fridge for several weeks.)

When choosing a site for your first angelica plant, it's important to remember that this stately creature can reach 2 metres in its second year. Once established, it doesn't like to be moved either – another reason to think carefully about where to put it. Its size and spread mean it's not ideal for containers.

Angelica likes a fairly shady situation and deep, fairly moist, but well-drained soil. Water it frequently until it's well established, and thereafter in dry spells.

Angelica won't produce flowers during the first year, but should grow fairly dramatically, giving you plenty of leaves and tender stems. It will then die back over the winter and emerge in spring for a second year, when it should produce bonny, blowsy flowerheads. Sometimes this doesn't happen until the third or even fourth year. You can often persuade the plant to live longer by cutting off the flowers before the seeds develop. Seed formation signifies the beginning of the end for that particular plant but you can gather the seeds to start the next cycle.

The plant is very hardy so you can simply sow the seeds in autumn, soon after harvesting, straight into the ground. Alternatively, let the plant self-seed and transplant the seedlings if necessary, when still very small.

# Anise hyssop *Agastache foeniculum*

| PLANT GROUP | Hardy perennial |
| --- | --- |
| HARVEST | May–September |

This statuesque herb has a sweet, fresh minty aniseed flavour. It is also called liquorice mint, which tells you pretty much all you need to know. It's lovely with shellfish and has a delicate seasoning effect on sweet foods, not dissimilar to mint.

## In the kitchen

Anise hyssop is a herb to use fresh, rather than cooked. If you do cook it, do so only briefly. The leaves can be a little on the tough side, so always shred or chop them finely. You can use the blooms as well – pinch them into little flowerlets.

- Anise hyssop is really good chopped finely and combined with sliced strawberries and plenty of caster sugar. Try it sprinkled on peaches too.
- Try anise hyssop, finely chopped, sprinkled on seared scallops, cold cooked crab or prawns. Finish with a spritz of lemon juice.
- You can use it in place of mint in many recipes.
- Infuse a jar of warmed honey with anise hyssop leaves and flowers.
- Anise hyssop makes a delicate tea, very soothing after a meal.
- In small amounts, it's nice in mixed fresh herbs – in an omelette, for instance, or tossed with a knob of butter into just-cooked carrots or peas.

## How to grow

This hardy perennial can be grown from seed but it needs warmth to germinate. Put your plug trays in a warm spot indoors, or sow outdoors in summer, using horticultural fleece or a cloche to protect seedlings in cold weather. Young plants for spring and summer planting are easy to buy from a specialist herb-grower.

Anise hyssop likes rich soil and full sun, where its waving brush-like flowers can soak up the light. It grows tall and upright so it looks great at the back of a bed, against a sunny wall or fence. It should produce its purple-blue blooms in mid to late summer. Pinch out the flowers to maintain good leaf production (they can be used in the kitchen), but leave some on in late summer to give the plant the chance to self-seed. Anise hyssop can be grown in a pot outdoors but you'll need a big one.

## Relatives

Korean mint (*Agastache rugosa*) can be used in similar ways but it's more pungently pepperminty, so I'd be cautious about using it in delicate savoury dishes.

# Basil _Ocimum basilicum_

| PLANT GROUP | Half-hardy annual |
|---|---|
| HARVEST | June–September |

Glorious basil, fragrant almost to a fault, has a unique honeyed, aniseedy pungency that becomes quite addictive. As long as you remember the golden rule – don't actually _cook_ it – it's a fabulous herb in the kitchen. Basil has many gorgeous manifestations (see overleaf) but the classic green 'Sweet Genovese' variety is an absolute essential for so many good things: a simple caprese salad with tomato and mozzarella, a piquant pesto, the ultimate chicken sandwich and a thousand different pasta dishes, to name but a few. It's also exquisite in some sweet dishes, such as ice creams or truffles.

## In the kitchen

Where shall I start? Basil can enhance so many things. The important point, as I've said, is to cook it very little or not at all. It's best torn or shredded and added raw, right at the end, just lightly stirred into a dish or simply scattered on top. Long cooking and intense heat will render it undetectable. There are rumours put about that you should only ever tear basil, not cut it. It certainly looks pretty when torn, but a finely sliced chiffonade (see p.18), or a processor-blitzed pesto should convince you that a knife blade will not somehow steal its flavour. I generally only use the leaves, but you can use the stalks to infuse flavour in a cream or a soup. They are a bit tough and slightly bitter for straight eating.

- Basil is lovely in salads, and particularly good with tomatoes, cucumber, grilled or sautéed courgettes or aubergine, peppers and mild salty cheeses such as halloumi or a firm goat's cheese.
- Basil works well with soft fruit too. Toss it with sliced, sugared strawberries or a fresh peach and blueberry salad.
- Add basil to any lemony dressing or sauce, including mayonnaise (p.159).
- This herb is delicious on soups – particularly pea or bean soups, gazpacho, or any kind of light chicken broth.
- I love to throw a handful of roughly chopped basil into veg and pasta combinations just before serving – such as broccoli, garlic and chilli.
- **Basil and parsley pesto** (p.166)
- **Herb noodle soup** (p.173)
- **Raspberry ripple basil ice cream** (p.219)
- **White chocolate truffles with basil** (p.229)

Basil *Ocimum basilicum* 'Sweet Genovese'

Thai basil *Ocimum basilicum* 'Horapha'

## How to grow

Basil is not entirely without trial for the gardener. It's a bit fussy and it likes warmth – not surprisingly, since it came originally from Asia.

Generally, I'd say basil is a herb to raise from seed, with successional sowings, so you can produce lots of it, and to grow in a pot so you can more easily control its environment. You can also try the guttering approach (p.33).

This is very much a summer herb – to enjoy from around June to September. Sow in late spring, cosseting your basil in a greenhouse, a sunny conservatory or kitchen or a very warm, sheltered bit of garden. While it loves the sun, it does not like to dry out – in fact, it likes a humid environment and rich, moist soil.

Keep a daily check on your basil plants for any sign of wilting. Water them from the base, pouring water into the tray they're sitting in, to encourage roots downwards. Water early in the day, not the evening. If you do have your basil outside, bring it indoors if the weather is less than warm – say, 18°C or lower in the daytime. You should certainly bring it in if it drops to 5°C or lower at night. Pinch out the growing tips and flowers to encourage bushy, tender growth and the best flavour.

## Varieties

**Thai basil (*Ocimum basilicum* 'Horapha')** Also just known as horapha, this tastes really very different to classic sweet basil, though it is related. I love it. Ridiculously aniseedy – almost liquorice-like – it's a wonderful pungent addition to curries, laksas and spicy soups (such as the one on p.173).

**Greek basil or bush basil (*Ocimum basilicum* var. *minimum*)** This has small leaves, which, perhaps due to their Latin name, seem to have an inferiority complex that they tackle by veritably yelling with flavour. This basil is great sprinkled liberally on top of stews or meaty soups at the last minute.

**Purple basil (*Ocimum basilicum* var. *purpurascens*)** This looks stunning, but doesn't have quite the same purity and pungency of flavour as good old green basil and is harder to grow.

**Holy basil (*Ocimum basilicum sanctum*)** This has an intense, slightly minty flavour and is often used in Thai cooking.

Then there's lemon basil, cinnamon basil, lime basil and tempting exotic spicy varieties such as 'Spicy Globe' and 'Siam Queen'. Most of these are hard to buy as fresh herbs, but you can easily source the seeds for a huge range of basils (see Directory, p.248). So, if you have a greenhouse or, at least, a capacious windowsill or two, experiment away.

# Bay *Laurus nobilis*

| PLANT GROUP | Perennial evergreen |
|---|---|
| HARVEST | All year round |

I love bay. Its scent – of lemon and new-split wood and smoke and roses – transports me to a place of safety. I use it almost every day and it would be my desert island herb because it is so deep and rich in flavour and so incredibly versatile. I associate bay with that culinary moment when a dish is assembled but not yet complete – the torn or twisted leaf, dropped into the stockpot, the roasting dish or the milk pan, is like a signal for the magic to begin.

## In the kitchen

Bay ranks alongside salt, pepper and lemons as an essential everyday seasoning. It enhances and underlines, rather than dominates, and gives a warm, earthy base note to everything it's cooked with – a little citrusy, a little resinous. It can be just as lovely in a sweet dish as a savoury one. You have to unlock its flavour with heat and, usually, with infusion in a liquid – hence the success of simmering it in stews, stocks and sauces, soups, custards or syrups. Having said that, bay leaves simply added to the skewer for barbecue kebabs, or thrown into a pan before frying fish or a chunk of meat, will still give up their lovely perfume. However I use bay, I always tease the essential oils out a little by damaging the leaf in some way – a twist, a tear or a quick whack with a pestle. One or two leaves is usually enough in most dishes, but add more if you like. It's quite hard to overuse the herb because you don't eat the leaves themselves (they are tough and bitter) but rather capture their flavour in another medium.

- Bay is essential to the classic bouquet garni (see p.19), which gives flavour to many a stew. Tie a couple of leaves together with a good sprig of thyme and some parsley stalks, adding a strip of leek or celery for extra flavour.
- Add bay to oil-based marinades – try shredding the leaves finely first to maximise flavour transfer.
- There are very few soups that don't benefit from a bay leaf or two added before cooking, but do remember to remove them before puréeing or you'll have a soup full of tough little leaf scraps (obviously, I've never done this myself...)
- Bay is used in Indian cooking, typically added to hot oil with other spices in the early stages of a dish.
- Never make any kind of stock without at least one bay leaf. Just don't.

- Whenever you're heating milk for a béchamel or cheese sauce, add a bay leaf too. A halved onion and a few peppercorns further add to the subtle savoury flavour.
- Try using bay liberally with fish: stuff it inside a fish before baking, add it to the pan when frying, or make a bed of the leaves for the fish to bake on. Throw bay on to a barbecue before grilling fish too.
- Bay always adds something to a tomato sauce, and to tomato-based dishes such as bolognese or chilli.
- Add a twisted bay leaf to a rice pudding before baking, in place of the more usual vanilla pod.
- Use bay to scent a syrup for poaching fruit, such as pears.
- Tear the fleshy parts of a few bay leaves away from their central stalks. Using a pestle and mortar, pound and crush with either a measure of granulated sugar or flaky sea salt to a green powder. Add bay sugar to a fruit pie filling; use bay salt as part of a rub for meat before cooking.
- If you have plenty of bay to spare, try throwing a leafy twig or two on to barbecue coals to create a wonderfully fragrant smoke.
- **White beans with winter herbs** (p.204)
- **Herb ice cream** (p.219)

## How to grow

It is possible to buy bay seeds but growing a productive bush from scratch would be a lengthy and possibly frustrating process. Much better to invest in a small bay shrub and plant it in a large pot or a sunny patch of garden. It should provide you with many years' continuous harvest.

Bay is a native of southern Europe so, although it is just about frost-hardy, it doesn't like the cold or the wet – young plants especially. Aim to give it warmth, free-draining gritty soil and as much shelter from wind and frost as you can manage. It will grow well in a large pot, and this tactic enables you to keep it protected from the worst of the weather, even bringing it inside during winter when the shrub is still young.

As the tree matures, it tends to become tougher and hardier, so you can plant it out. In the right conditions, if nothing gets in its way, it will simply keep growing – unchecked bay trees can be several metres high.

Infusing milk for a béchamel sauce with bay

# Bergamot *Monarda didyma*

| PLANT GROUP | Hardy perennial |
| --- | --- |
| HARVEST | April–August |

Spectacular as it grows, this lovely pungent herb is a member of the mint family, though with its strong citrusy flavour, it reminds me most of marjoram. Note that the herb is not related to the bergamot orange (*Citrus aurantium bergamia*), whose aromatic oil gives Earl Grey tea its distinctive fragrance. However, you can use the herb to make a very nice tea of its own (see p.244), or put a good sprig into black tea while it brews, for a refreshing, warming, slightly resinous extra layer of flavour.

## In the kitchen
Bergamot ranks close to thyme, rosemary, marjoram and the savories as a punchy, aromatic all-rounder. As it's quite strong, start with a little and work your way up.

- Stir chopped bergamot into roasted squash as soon as it comes out of the oven, or blend into a roasted squash soup.
- Bergamot is a good addition when fresh mixed herbs are called for in a recipe – combine it with parsley, thyme or tarragon.
- Try substituting bergamot for oregano or marjoram in almost any recipe.
- **Bergamot scones** (p.215)

## How to grow
Bergamot grows well from seed but it needs plenty of warmth to germinate and is best sown indoors. Or you can buy a few young plants for late-spring or summer planting. Bergamot is tall and slightly spindly so several plants together look best. It is not an obvious choice for containers, but should grow well in a large, deep one. The plants like sun or partial shade and rich, moist, but not wet, soil; don't let them dry out. The leaves will taste best before flowering in mid to late summer, but do let those flowers come because the plant will attract lots of bees.

Although this herb is a perennial and should give you little trouble once established, it's best to dig up the plant after 2 or 3 years and remove the centre, then replant the younger outer parts.

## Relatives
Lemon bergamot (*Monarda citriodora*) is an annual which also has flamboyant blooms. The leaves have a strong lemon flavour. Wild bergamot (*Monarda fistulosa*) is very strong and more often used medicinally or as a tea than for eating.

# Borage *Borago officinalis*

| PLANT GROUP | Hardy annual |
| --- | --- |
| HARVEST | April–October |

Borage, for me, is all about the flowers. Some greengrocers and supermarkets now sell it, but I would highly recommend growing this herb yourself so you can harvest plenty of its gorgeous, delicate and delicious blooms. They look beautiful scattered on puddings, cakes, or salads (sweet or savoury) and are lovely dropped into drinks. When you eat them, they pop in the mouth, releasing a little bead of refreshing, sweet, delicately cucumbery juice. Borage is a handsome plant, and easy to grow – what's not to like?

## In the kitchen
Borage leaves are traditionally cooked as a vegetable or used as a herb in various European cultures. However, I find their thick, hairy, coarse texture off-putting, even when they are young. And their very mild cucumber taste doesn't do an awful lot for me. That said, I have found the finely chopped young leaves are a good way to flavour crème fraîche (see below).

Don't take my word for it, though – if you're growing borage for its flowers, you might as well try the leaves too. I would, however, strongly recommend chopping them up pretty finely.

- To make borage and smoked salmon canapés, stir a good 2 tbsp finely chopped young borage leaves into 200ml crème fraîche. Season lightly with salt and pepper. Put small dollops of the mixture on top of crostini or squares of brown toast, add a curl of smoked salmon, and garnish with a borage flower.
- Put borage flowers into ice-cube trays, top up with water and freeze. These ice cubes are beautiful in summer drinks (see p.240).
- Borage is, of course, a key ingredient in the classic Pimms cocktail – often replaced, but never bettered, by a bit of cucumber.
- I would scatter borage flowers on almost any kind of salad, but they are particularly good on strawberries or raspberries, and with savoury ingredients such as chicken and soft goat's cheeses that pair naturally well with cucumber.
- Use to finish off cucumber dishes, salads and soups in particular.
- **Simple herb salad** (p.175)
- **Sorrel wine cup** (p.243)

## How to grow

This herb is very easy to raise from seed. Sow directly in the garden – try a couple of sowings through spring and summer for lots of flowers. You can also start borage off in plugs but it grows fast, so transplant before it gets too big. The plant can reach 1 metre in height and has a deep root. I wouldn't choose it as a container plant because of its fast-growing, expansive nature.

Borage isn't too fussy about where it grows, though it likes sun and open sandy free-draining soil if possible. It should give you blooms from early summer through to autumn. Deadhead it to prolong flowering, but leave some flowers late in the season if you want it to self-seed, which it will readily do – I've found it's happy to spread itself about the garden with no help from me.

*Borago officinalis* has blue flowers, and the plants sometimes produce random pink ones too. You can also buy *Borago officinalis* 'Alba', which blooms white and is equally pretty. The flowers are rich in nectar and bees absolutely love them – so much so that one fetching old name for this herb is 'bee bread'. Pale, delicate borage honey is well worth seeking out.

Borage is believed to be a friendly companion plant to tomatoes, legumes, brassicas and strawberries, luring away bugs and mysteriously improving the flavour of the fruit or vegetable.

# Caraway *Carum carvi*

| PLANT GROUP | Hardy biennial |
|---|---|
| HARVEST | Leaves: May–June |
| | Seeds: September–October of the second year |

This delicious plant is really used more as a spice than a herb. You can eat caraway leaves – they have a pleasant, parsley-ish flavour – but they're not really anything to write home about. Caraway is best known for its seed, and understandably so. The long, gently curved brown seeds are packed with a distinctive warm, spicy, nutty-sweet flavour.

## In the kitchen

Caraway seed is one of those flavours that works equally well in sweet and savoury applications. While my favourite way to enjoy it is in cakes and puddings, it goes incredibly well with cabbages, beans and other greens, as well as meats and cheeses. As with most seeds, the flavour is maximised if you use it relatively fresh, toast it very lightly in a dry frying pan, then crush, grind or pound it in a spice mill or with a pestle and mortar.

- Caraway enhances many a spice mix, including the North African merguez blend: toast equal quantities of caraway, cumin, fennel and coriander seeds and black peppercorns in a dry frying pan, then crush with a pestle and mortar. Use the blend in a stew, soup or tagine, stir into a hot chickpea salad with plenty of olive oil and lemon juice, or blend with crushed garlic, salt and oil to make a delicious rub for a joint of meat.

- Fiery harissa paste, also North African, needs caraway too. Recipes vary but usually include the four 'c's – chilli, cumin, coriander and caraway – blended with olive oil, garlic and sometimes tomatoes. A teaspoonful will transform bland rice or couscous dishes, or it can be thinned with a little more oil to make a delicious swirl on houmous or a vegetable soup.

- Caraway is the seed in good old-fashioned seed cake: simply add 2–3 tsp to any Victoria sponge, pound cake or Madeira cake recipe to enjoy the effect. It's also excellent in biscuits – try it in the recipe on p.225.

- Mix a little crushed caraway with cooking apples and sugar for a pie or crumble. Or stuff a pinch into the centre of an apple before baking, with some butter and brown sugar. It goes with plums, apricots and pears too.

- Toss lightly toasted caraway into steamed or stir-fried cabbage, kale, Brussels sprouts or other greens to lift and sweeten their earthy flavour.

## How to grow

Raising caraway for your own seed harvest is, to some extent, a labour of love because you have to wait for its second year before the seed forms, and you would need several plants to yield more than a few tablespoonfuls of seed. However, caraway is not hard to grow and I do think that freshly harvested seeds – of this and other herbs with fragrant seeds, such as fennel, celery leaf and coriander – really have the edge on flavour.

Growing caraway from seed is straightforward and an economical way to grow lots of plants. It has a long tap root and is not ideal for containers. Instead, sow the seeds straight into weed-free ground, in a sheltered, sunny place. They really need warmth to germinate and grow, so late spring or early summer is the best time. You can also sow in late summer or early autumn. Thin out the seedlings once they are established to ensure a good healthy crop.

The plants will flower in their second summer and you can collect the seeds in late summer or early autumn once they are dry and look brown. Cut the seed heads in the middle of the day when there is no moisture on them. Keep the heads in a bowl or paper bag, in a dry place, for a week or two, then just pull or shake the seeds off. Store them in an airtight jar in a cool, dark cupboard.

Caraway seeds

# Celery leaf *Apium graveolens*

| PLANT GROUP | Hardy biennial |
| --- | --- |
| HARVEST | Leaves and stems: Any time in the first year |
| | Seeds: September–October of the second year |

Also known as cutting celery, wild celery or, rather charmingly, smallage, this is the plant from which our familiar thick-stemmed salad celery was originally bred, and knobbly-rooted celeriac too. The herb has all the marvellous earthy, peppery savour of those vegetables, and can be used to add a deep note of flavour to dishes in much the same way. Indeed, if you grow celery leaf, you will probably find that you have far less call on conventional celery. Easy to grow and very pretty too, I'd put it in any herb patch.

## In the kitchen
Celery leaf is quite pungent and slightly bitter so I'd suggest using it sparingly, adding more if you see fit. You can use the stems as well as the leaves. Added at the beginning of cooking, celery leaf will contribute a background note of savoury flavour. Keep it back until the last minute, or have it raw if you want a more defined peppery kick. The tiny, delicately ridged seeds have a delicious celery flavour too.

- Add a few roughly chopped leaves to a simple cheese sandwich, or combine with grated cheese for cheese on toast or a rarebit.
- Add a good sprig to any stock, or sweat down about 1 tbsp finely chopped leaves and stems with onions and garlic as the base for almost any soup.
- Celery leaf makes a very good addition to a pork and apple stuffing.
- Celery seeds have a strong nutty, slightly spicy flavour. They're so tiny that you can use them whole, or toast very lightly and roughly bash using a pestle and mortar to really maximise flavour. They're great added to a spice mix for a curry, pickle or chutney, delicious in breads (try in the recipe on p.211) and lend flavour to sweating onions for the base of a soup.
- **Celery leaf and lovage soup** (p.172)
- **Apple and celery leaf salad with Cheddar and walnuts** (p.175)

## How to grow
You can grow celery leaf easily from seed, sowing it in plug trays in early spring, or straight into the ground a bit later on.

In the wild, celery leaf often grows in marshy ground. It's a plant that likes to be kept moist and it will wilt somewhat alarmingly if it doesn't get enough water.

Rich, well-fed soil in a not-too-sunny position is best. I have also grown celery leaf very successfully in large containers.

If kept in a reasonably sheltered spot, and assuming you don't experience sub-arctic temperatures, a first-year celery leaf plant should give you a harvest of fresh leaves and stems right through the winter. In its second summer, it will flower. Cut back the flowers straight away if you want to keep a crop of leaves going, but leave them if you want to harvest the seed. If you want to do both, grow more than one plant, perhaps planting one each year to maximise production.

When the flowers have faded and the green-yellow seeds have ripened and look dry and a light dun colour, snip the seed heads off the plant. Keep the heads in a bowl or paper bag, in a dry place, for a week or two. I find it easiest to simply pinch and rub the tiny seeds off the stalks, on to a large white plate. Any unwanted bits of plant matter can be picked out with your fingers and you should be left with a cache of perfect little seeds. You can put them in a fine sieve and shake it to get rid of little bits of husk and dust, but some of the smaller seeds may pass through too.

Keep your seeds in an airtight container in a cool, dark place and use within a year. You won't get a great volume of seed from each plant, but what you do get will taste wonderful.

# Chervil *Anthriscus cerefolium*

| PLANT GROUP | Hardy annual |
| --- | --- |
| HARVEST | All year round |

Sweet, grassy, tender and delicately aniseedy, this is the most summery and salady of herbs, though it's possible to grow it right through the winter too. You can eat it raw by the forkful without feeling overpowered by it, and it subtly enhances all sorts of other flavours, particularly eggs, fish, green vegetables and chicken. Fine and feathery chervil is also one of the most beautiful edible leaves. It's lovely as a delicate garnish – just a couple of leaves floating on a soup, say.

As a herb though, it's one to use in quantity and as freshly picked as possible, so growing your own is a good idea. It grows easily from seed and, if you make successional sowings every few weeks from about March onwards, you should have a flourishing crop for most of the year. Chervil is also a herb that's fairly easy to buy, but it's hard to know whether the flavour will be good or not.

## In the kitchen

Use chervil fresh, raw and generously. Think of it both as a delicate herb and a salad leaf. Add a few sprigs to almost any green salad for a light seasoning effect, or, for more of a chervil hit, make it the base of the dish, along with some mild leaves such as lamb's lettuce. Add one or two other ingredients – blanched green beans or broad beans, asparagus, new potatoes, tomatoes, oranges, cold chicken, hard-boiled eggs, a few toasted seeds – and dress lightly with a simple vinaigrette. If you are going to cook chervil, do so very briefly.

- Combined in roughly equal quantities with tarragon, parsley and chives, chervil is an essential part of *fines herbes*, the classic French blend which is so good in an omelette or stirred into a creamy sauce for chicken or fish.
- Chop chervil fairly finely and stir it into homemade mayonnaise (p.159), with a little grated lemon zest – lovely with crab or other seafood.
- Stir at the last minute into a bowl of just-boiled new potatoes.
- Add chervil to just-cooked carrots, along with a knob of unsalted butter, a squeeze of lemon and lots of pepper. Serve as they are or blitz into a buttery purée.
- Make a simple salad of cooked, dressed Puy lentils, crumbled goat's cheese and quartered cherry tomatoes. Toss lots of chervil through it, and finish off with a bit more on top.
- **Chervil soup** (p.170)

- Chervil and lemon zest mayonnaise (p.159)
- Béarnaise sauce (p.160)
- Simple herb salad (p.175)
- Crab and broad bean salad (p.176)
- Herb omelette (p.182)

## How to grow

Given that there's not much point mucking about with chervil in piddly quantities, it's more economical to grow lots of it from seed, sowing two or three times through the year, than to buy loads of plants.

In early spring or autumn, sow chervil in plug trays or guttering (see p.33), then, once the seedlings look robust, transfer them to a bed or large pots in a lightly shaded spot outdoors. Rich, moisture-retaining soil is ideal. In warm weather, sow it straight into the ground – the seedlings prefer not to be moved.

To encourage constant new leafy growth, keep harvesting chervil, cutting any flowering stems right back, and watering well. Too much sun and too little water can make it flower quickly, then you lose the leaves. In a sheltered position, chervil should give leaves all through the winter.

Chives *Allium schoenoprasum* 'Corsican White'

# Chives *Allium schoenoprasum*

| PLANT GROUP | Hardy perennial |
|---|---|
| HARVEST | April–October |

This is not a herb I would ever want to be without, and it's immeasurably better when freshly snipped. The true flavour of chives is really quite punchy, a deep allium hit – but it fades incredibly quickly, so doesn't survive well when packaged and chilled. A pot of chives on your windowsill will stand you in good stead for all manner of salady, sandwichy applications. But if you can stretch to a lovely wild-haired clump or two growing in the garden, you'll be even better off.

One of the great things about growing your own chives is having the opportunity to use the flowers (see below). I wouldn't want to eat a whole one – a strange and overpowering mouthful that would be. But if you pinch out the little flowerlets with your fingertips, you have a handful of tiny oniony taste-bombs.

## In the kitchen

Harvest your chives by cropping them close to the earth. To chop them, use a very sharp, heavy knife or scissors (often easier), holding the chives together in a bundle on your chopping board (or in your hand if using scissors) and starting at the base. Chives are best used raw or very lightly cooked. I like them in an omelette or with scrambled eggs, but they really come into their own in salads. Combined with mayonnaise, oil or any kind of vinaigrette, they enliven and enhance lettuces and greens, potatoes, chicken, fish, eggs, beans, tomatoes, other alliums, squashes... the list goes on.

- Tiny pinched-out chive flowerlets are wonderful scattered on salads, savoury tarts or pizzas, in sandwich fillings, or used to finish a soup.
- For a lovely supper, bake some potatoes, then scoop out the soft flesh. Mash it with a knob of butter, some scraps of ham or cooked bacon and lots of snipped chives and/or chive flowers. Season with salt and pepper then pack back into the potato skins and return to the oven until crisp.
- For a delicious smoked mackerel and chive pâté, blitz 250g skinned, de-boned hot-smoked mackerel in a processor with 1 tsp English mustard, 2 tbsp crème fraîche, 2–3 tbsp snipped chives, some salt, pepper and lemon juice. Very good on oatcakes or brown toast.
- To make the simplest of chive sauces, just stir lots of the chopped herb into warmed crème fraîche. Season with salt, pepper and a squeeze of lemon and serve with fish or chicken and simply cooked veg.

Chives in flower

- **Chive mayonnaise** (p.159)
- **Simple herb salad** (p.175)
- **Herb omelette** (p.182)

## How to grow

You will probably find it easiest to buy baby chive plants or divide established ones, but you can grow this herb from seed. It needs warmth to germinate so start it off in spring in plug trays on a warm windowsill or in a heated greenhouse.

Once planted out, chives aren't overly fussy but prefer a rich, moist soil and plenty of sun. It's a good idea to prepare the ground with compost or manure before planting.

Once chives begin to flower, the stems harden and their flavour diminishes so you need to remove the flowering stems to get optimum tender chivey growth. My approach is to cut flowering stems right down at the base, then use some of the flowers. Standard chives have purple flowers but you can get very pretty white and variegated varieties too. Once the flowers are coming thick and fast, or you've used up most of the clump, cut it right back, almost to the ground. Sprinkle a little earth over the plant, water it well and you should get a thriving second crop; repeat and you'll get a third or even fourth, taking you right through to autumn. Allow the last of the leaves to die back naturally – these will feed the bulbs underground. Chives grow well in pots but keep watering.

You get the best flavour from one- or two-year-old plants, so replace regularly. You can divide the roots of existing plants by carefully digging them up in spring or autumn, pulling the bulb cluster apart and replanting.

Chives are good companion plants. Their scent deters carrot fly and, like other alliums, they are a useful partner for roses, helping to protect them from both greenfly and fungal diseases.

## Relatives

Garlic chives (*Allium tuberosum*) are delicious flat-leaved, white-flowered relatives of standard chives. You can use them in much the same way, and they contribute a subtly more garlicky savour. If you grow any, make sure you let at least some of them flower. They are larger and more statuesque than ordinary chives and their beautiful white blooms – lots of little ones clustered together into one gorgeous umbel – are absolutely fantastic to eat. If you can bear to remove them from the garden, scatter them on salads, just-cooked pizza or roasted red peppers, or use them in an omelette (see p.182).

# Coriander *Coriandrum sativum*

| PLANT GROUP | Hardy annual |
|---|---|
| HARVEST | Leaves: May–September |
| | Seeds: September–October |

This pretty, delicate, lacy herb, which is also known as cilantro, has a unique character yet it's incredibly versatile and very widely used. That hard-to-define flavour is sweet, astringent, citrusy, cleansing and somehow perfumed, all at the same time. Cooks have been adding coriander to dishes for thousands of years and its dominion is broad. It is, as the wonderful vegetarian cookery writer Nadine Abensur writes, part of 'the joys of almost all cooking outside Europe'. You'll find it used widely in so many cuisines, including Indian, Thai, Chinese, Portuguese, North African, Middle Eastern and Mexican, and within these you'll discover how deliciously well it partners spices, garlic, ginger and, above all, chilli – the cooling, fragrant foil to the fire.

## In the kitchen

Coriander is a deeply aromatic herb that can give enormous character to a dish. It's best used very fresh, and in quantity. Some recipes – most notably curries, where it is often added in huge handfuls – call for coriander to be added during cooking, but the flavour does dissipate. It is most often added at the end of cooking, or sprinkled on generously before serving. You can add the more tender parts of the stalks to dishes as well as the leaves, but they do need to be chopped finely.

If you are among those who really don't enjoy the flavour of coriander, then basil or mint, or a combination of the two, can be successful alternatives.

- **Chermoula** Based around coriander, chilli and garlic, this fabulous rich and spicy North African sauce is traditionally served with fish but it's also delicious with chicken, lamb and grilled or roasted vegetables. Or you can serve it as a side dip to a mezze-style spread of salads and breads, or add a swirl to a dish of houmous. Either serve it raw or add to a cooked dish. To make chermoula, finely chop 2 garlic cloves on a large board. Finely chop 1 deseeded green chilli and add to the garlic. Add the leaves from a large bunch of coriander and a slightly smaller bunch of flat-leaf parsley. Now chop together as finely as you can (see p.18). Transfer to a bowl and stir in 1 tsp sweet smoked paprika, 1 tsp ground cumin, the juice and zest of ½ lemon and enough olive oil to make a thick paste (around 150ml). Season with salt, pepper and a pinch of sugar.

Coriander seedlings

- Add at the last minute to laksas and noodle soups – keep the leaves whole so they can float, flower-like, in the broth.
- Use coriander in homemade Thai curry pastes. Even if you 'cheat' and use a good ready-made curry paste (which I frequently do), a generous snowfall of fresh chopped coriander will finish the dish very nicely.
- Coriander is essential in guacamole.
- For a lovely simple salsa, chop about 250g tomatoes (green tomatoes or tomatilloes if you have them, though red are fine too). Toss lightly with a deseeded and finely chopped green chilli, a chopped large bunch of coriander, 1 tbsp olive oil, the juice and grated zest of ½ lime and a good pinch each of salt and sugar. This is also very good if you add snipped chives or little chive flowerlets. Delicious with burgers or alongside a chilli.
- Coriander is brilliant in rice or noodle salads with other big flavours, such as lime juice, garlic and toasted cumin seeds.
- Coriander seed has a wonderful warm spice flavour, quite different from the leaves. If you grow your own, you can use the seed when it is still green and fresh – roughly crush and add to curries, stews or dressings. The dried seed has countless uses, from curries and tagines to preserves and cakes. It is usually included in proprietary 'mixed spice' blends too.
- **Herby chicken noodle salad** (p.179)
- **Herb noodle soup** (p.173)

## How to grow

As a fast grower that you're likely to want to use in quantity, this is a herb to raise from seed. Sow directly into the growing site as it dislikes being moved. It grows well in a container too, but choose a fairly deep one to accommodate the tap root.

Coriander can go from a mass of lush leaves to a leggy, flowery, seedy thing in an alarmingly short space of time. To keep it leafy and kitchen-friendly, let it see some sun but not too much – if grown in a heat-trap, it may seed quickly. Give it lightish, well-drained soil but plenty of water – don't let the soil dry out. And, most importantly, keep cutting the leaves. Even with these provisos, it will still run to seed relatively quickly. Sow successively from April/May onwards to guarantee a good supply of this lovely herb all through summer and into the autumn.

Don't chuck away your seedy plants: the seeds are all part of coriander's appeal. When they are still just fat green berries, they have the most amazing fresh spice flavour. Alternatively, leave them on the plant until dry and beige, and they can be harvested and stored in the same way as other herb seeds, such as caraway (see p.57).

Coriander is one herb that responds very well to the 'micro-leafing' approach (see p.33) and this means you can enjoy its flavour without worrying about the whole bolting/going to seed issue.

# Dill *Anethum graveolens*

| PLANT GROUP | Hardy annual |
|---|---|
| HARVEST | Leaves: May–September |
| | Seeds: September–October |

Pungent, fresh, aniseedy, this is an assertive herb but one that's easy to fall in love with. In looks, taste and application, it has something in common with fennel, but is by no means the same, being rather more penetrating and astringent.

## In the kitchen

Dill doesn't respond well to long cooking but is fabulous raw and can stand up to really big flavours such as smoked fish, beetroot, mustard and onions. It's quite a deep, lingering taste and you don't necessarily need a huge amount of it, but, nevertheless, it can be effective if used in large quantities.

- Use scissors to snip dill over almost any fish dish before serving.
- Dill is lovely tossed with just-cooked broad beans or peas along with a snippet of unsalted butter.
- Stir lots of chopped dill into a mustardy mayonnaise (see p.159) to serve with green salads, beetroot, cucumber, eggs, fish or chicken.
- For a tasty canapé, mix 100g cream cheese or mild soft goat's cheese with 1 tbsp chopped dill, 2 tsp rinsed baby capers, a squeeze of lemon juice and plenty of pepper. Spread thickly on squares of rye bread and top with a curl of smoked trout. Or use the combination as a sandwich filling.
- For a cucumber salad, peel 1 large cucumber, halve lengthways, scoop out the seeds and slice thickly. Toss with 1 tsp cider vinegar, 1 tbsp rapeseed or olive oil, a pinch each of salt, sugar and pepper and 1 tbsp chopped dill.
- Dill seed has a warm anise-tinged flavour and is a traditional pickling spice.
- **Potato salad with dill and pickled red onion** (p.181)
- **Carrot soup with dill and mustard** (p.169)

## How to grow

Dill is easy to grow from seed and is best sown directly into the ground or a pot as it doesn't like being moved. Sow several times during the spring and summer for a good supply. Site well away from any fennel plants as the two can cross-pollinate.

Dill favours a light, well-drained soil in sun or partial shade. Keep it well watered, remove any flower stems and keep cutting the leaves. Once the plant has gone to seed (it will, eventually), let the seeds ripen, then harvest as for caraway (see p.57).

# Fennel *Foeniculum vulgare*

| PLANT GROUP | Hardy perennial |
|---|---|
| HARVEST | Leaves: May–September |
| | Seeds: September–October |

Fennel herb, which is available in green and bronze varieties, is not the same as the tasty fat white bulb of the vegetable Florence fennel (*Foeniculum vulgare* var. *dulce*). You can grow Florence fennel and still take advantage of the leafy fronds – often if you buy a bulb it will have a few fronds still attached – but the flavour is not as punchy. The taste of a young, freshly picked frond of fennel herb is out of this world – intensely sweet and aniseedy, fragrant, almost floral.

Fennel seeds are also a delicious and unique seasoning, different from and more spicy than the leaves. They are easy to buy but, if you have a plant or two, you will be able to collect the ripe seeds yourself (see overleaf).

## In the kitchen

The sharp, sweet aniseed tang of fennel is lovely with rich foods such as lamb, pork, creamy vegetable soups or oil-rich breads. Fennel fronds can take a bit of heat but not too much – raw or lightly cooked is best. I always think it's worth chopping fennel pretty fine. Eating a whole frond, with its almost hair-like texture, is vaguely disconcerting. I find the flavour of green fennel to be slightly better than that of the bronze variety.

Fennel seeds are a whole other ingredient – much stronger and more penetrating than the leaf. Whether fresh and green or mature and dried, they can be roughly crushed or completely ground and make a marvellous addition to all sorts of spice mixes, to sauces, soups and dressings, to breads and some sweet dishes too.

- It's almost a cliché to serve fennel with fish – but, like most clichés, it has become one for a very good reason. Stuff fennel fronds generously inside fish before baking or, if you've got some juices from frying or roasting fish, enrich them with a little cream or butter and stir in lots of finely chopped fennel. Add fennel to a homemade fish stock or court bouillon (a delicately flavoured liquid often used for poaching fish).
- Chopped fennel works very well with tomatoes, too, and in a potato and/ or beetroot salad.
- Combine chopped fennel with soured cream or full-fat yoghurt, season well with salt and pepper and use alongside houmous and other dips, or mashed into a hot baked potato.

Fennel seeds

- Fennel herb always combines well with fennel bulb. Use the herb to enhance a salad of very finely sliced raw fennel bulb, dressed with olive oil, lemon juice, salt and pepper. Finish off with goat's cheese.
- For a lovely simple starter, cook some 'soft hard-boiled' eggs (7 minutes' boiling for a large egg at room temperature), peel and cut open while still warm. Pop a knob of butter on the yolks, add a grinding of pepper and scatter with lots of chopped fresh fennel and a few baby capers.
- **Double fennel braise** (p.207)
- **Fennel seed bread** (p.211)
- **Pasta with sardines and fennel** (p.187)
- **Pork with fennel and rosemary** (p.191)
- **Fennel fudge** (p.230)

## How to grow

Fennel herb, whether green or bronze, is a tall, handsome plant that will give structure and height to any herb or veg patch. It grows readily from seed – sow in early spring indoors, or outside a bit later on. (Keep it away from dill as the two may cross-pollinate.) Because of its stature, fennel is not one for indoor growing, though I have raised it successfully in a large, deep pot. It likes sun and rich, well-drained soil.

As with all herbs, not allowing it to flower will encourage lots of leafy growth. However, since the seeds of fennel are one of its great attractions, do leave some flowers, or keep a plant or two just for seed production.

Around September time, the fennel flowers will have faded and been replaced by umbels of plump little green berries. You can eat the seeds when still young and juicy like this – just chewing a few fresh from the plant is a lovely way to freshen the breath. But if you want to gather and store the dry seeds, wait until they have faded on the plant from bright green berries to little delicately striped, dun-coloured pellets. Don't let them get to the point where they turn black. If you nibble one it should give you a real shot of fresh, pungent fennely flavour, without mustiness. Cut the seed heads in the middle of the day when there is no moisture on them. Keep the heads in a bowl or a paper bag, in a dry place, for a week or two, then just pull the seeds off. Store them in an airtight jar in a cool, dark cupboard.

Cut back the spent stalks of your fennel plants in the winter. The plant will die right down and then reappear in spring. It self-seeds enthusiastically. Replace plants after 3 or 4 years.

Garlic prepared for roasting

# Garlic *Allium sativum*

| PLANT GROUP | Hardy perennial grown as an annual |
|---|---|
| HARVEST | Green garlic: May–June |
| | Mature garlic: July–August |

There must be very few cooks who don't use garlic regularly: it is an almost indispensable flavouring with impressive versatility. Depending on the way you prepare and cook it, garlic can be a subtle and almost undetectable seasoning, or a loud-and-proud shout of flavour that dominates a dish, and pretty much anything in between.

It's not just mature garlic cloves you can use in the kitchen. Garlic 'scapes' are slender, curling flower stems taken from the young growing plant. You only get them with slightly less common 'hardneck' types of garlic, and they are hard to find unless you grow your own. However, if you do, they're very good when lightly cooked or used in a dressing or pesto.

Immature bulbs, or 'green garlic', harvested in spring, also make good eating. Tender and plump, the cloves within them are small and mild and can be used whole – sliced up rather like an onion, skin and all. Sweat them down as you would onions or leeks. They are very good in soups.

Mature garlic bulbs, with firm cloves and thin, papery skin, are at their peak shortly after harvesting, following a brief period of drying. As garlic is now imported from all over the world, you can usually find it in this peak condition at most times of the year. Garlic grown in Britain tends to be at its best during late summer.

As garlic ages in storage, the cloves start to soften and shrink a little and soft green shoots begin to germinate at their hearts. Garlic like this is no longer at its best and is heading towards bitterness. You can discard any incipient baby shoots from the middle of the cloves and still use the rest of them, but garlic that is clearly shooting is not good for eating.

Storing garlic in the fridge isn't advised because chilling affects the flavour, making it less intense. In addition, garlic stored at very low temperatures may start shooting (it's cold weather that stimulates growth in the plant). Really, you want to store garlic in a cool, dry place, with some air circulation around the bulbs, so hanging it in a cool larder would be ideal. If you don't have these conditions, then brief storage in the fridge is probably preferable to a warm and/or humid kitchen.

## In the kitchen

Your kitchen knife calls the shots when it comes to getting the right results from garlic. For basic peeling, crushing and chopping techniques, see p.20.

- **Crushed garlic** Crushing garlic breaks down the cell membranes and releases compounds that deliver garlicky flavour at its most intense and ferocious. Hot and strong it may be, but this is a wonderful flavouring ingredient. Use it to add piquancy to a mayonnaise or dressing, to beat into butter, or to add to any dish where you want a powerful and persistent garlic flavour.
- **Chopped garlic** Chop garlic finely and you'll get a significant garlicky flavour, without the heat and pungency of the crushed clove. Chopped garlic can be very good raw if it's used in small quantities and combined with other ingredients – gremolata (overleaf) is the perfect example – but it is most often cooked. I like to add finely chopped garlic to a pasta dish, stir-fry or soup right at the end of cooking, giving it only a minute or two's heating. This is just enough to take the sharp edge off the garlic without diminishing its penetrating flavour. Chopped garlic added at the beginning of cooking will lend a more gentle but nonetheless notable sweet pungent note to a dish.
- **Slivered garlic** Finely slivered garlic always seems to me a little more subtle than chopped. It's particularly good gently infused in hot oil before trickling on a pizza or freshly baked focaccia, or in a dish such as pasta aglio e olio (see overleaf).
- **Whole roasted garlic** Keep garlic cloves whole and unpeeled and roast them until soft, and you have a whole different flavour again: sweet, mellow and mild. To roast a bulb whole, cut off the tip of the bulb to just expose the cloves, then put it on a piece of foil, trickle with olive or rapeseed oil and seal the foil loosely. Bake at 190°C/Gas mark 5 for about 45 minutes, or until the cloves are really soft. Alternatively, release the cloves from the bulb and toss them with chopped veg before roasting. Soft roasted garlic is good smeared on bruschetta or blended into soups or just squeezed from its skin and smudged all over the veg or meat you've roasted it with.

Always remember that garlic, which is rich in sugars, burns very easily. Put it in a pan on too high a heat and you'll get a brown, bitter result in no time. You need to cook it gently and protect it. This can be done by adding salt to draw the juice out of the garlic, helping it sweat rather than sear, or by combining it with other ingredients, such as onions, cream or tomatoes, whose liquid will stop it burning.

There are a million and one recipes that use garlic as a crucial supporting player. There are rather fewer in which it is the star of the show but these include some real corkers – do try chicken with forty cloves of garlic (p.196). There are also everyday uses that I return to time and again.

Green garlic

- **Gremolata** This is simply finely chopped raw garlic, parsley and lemon zest, mixed together. Say, 1 clove of garlic, the zest of 1 lemon and 1 heaped tbsp chopped parsley. The mix is traditionally strewn over the Italian dish of osso bucco (braised veal shanks). However, it can be good on almost any rich meat dish, as well as risottos, pasta dishes, fish, soups and roasted vegetables.
- **Garlic butter** Combine 250g softened unsalted butter with 3 finely crushed garlic cloves, 1 heaped tbsp finely chopped parsley, the finely grated zest of 1 lemon, and some salt and pepper. This gives you enough butter to make garlic bread with 1 large baguette, or to stuff under the skin of a large chicken before roasting, with a bit left over. You can also freeze it in a log, wrapped in cling film, to slice into thick discs for melting on grilled fish, steak or mushrooms – I think it's best with at least a little cooking, however, to soften the garlic a touch.
- **Chapon** This is simply a stale chunk of bread, rubbed all over with a cut clove of garlic, then tossed into a green salad. It imparts a delicate garlicky savour to the leaves. You're not meant to eat the actual chapon.
- **Pasta aglio e olio** This is one of the best answers I've ever come across to the old it's-late-and-I'm-hungry-and-there's-no-food-in-the-house dilemma. Put some pasta on to boil (spaghetti or linguine is best). Very gently warm 2–3 tbsp good olive oil in a small pan. Add 1–2 finely slivered cloves of garlic and either some chopped fresh red chilli or a good pinch of dried chilli flakes. Warm through so the garlic cooks a little but doesn't go beyond the palest yellow colour. Drain the cooked pasta, toss it in this garlicky oil, add some salt and pepper and dust with grated Parmesan. Pure satisfaction.
- **Bruschetta** This is toast at its finest. Toast a thick slice of good sourdough or other robust country-style bread. Cut a clove of garlic in half and rub the cut sides all over the hot rough surface of the bread. Trickle generously with extra virgin olive oil and sprinkle with salt. On its own, this is a lovely breakfast or snack, but of course you can top it with anything from fresh tomatoes to wilted kale, a poached egg or shaved Parmesan, grilled sardines or a thousand other things.
- **Skordalia** (p.165)
- **Parsley mayonnaise** (p.159)
- **Basil and parsley pesto** (p.166)
- **Salmoriglio sauce** (p.165)
- **Baked chicken with forty cloves of garlic** (p.196)
- **Pork with fennel and rosemary** (p.191)
- **White beans with winter herbs** (p.204)

# How to grow

Is it worth growing garlic when it's so readily available, and when most of us use it in large quantities? I'd say yes, if you've got a bit of room, and not least for the pure satisfaction of it. Growing your own enables you to try different varieties, to get your garlic very fresh, and gives you access to tender green garlic. And, if you choose a 'hardneck' variety, you'll be able to have tasty garlic scapes (see below).

In theory, you could simply take a few sprouting cloves from shop-bought garlic and plonk them in the soil. They would probably grow, but they would be prone to viruses. Varieties specifically bred for garden growing in our climate, such as 'Cristo', 'Albigensian Wight' or 'Solent Wight', will give you much better results. They prefer a sunny site and rich, well-drained soil; work in compost and also sand beforehand if you can. If you have an acid soil, below pH 6.5, you may have trouble growing garlic.

Most garlic is planted in autumn or early winter, although you can also find spring-planted varieties. After preparing your soil, press individual cloves, pointy end up, 5–10cm down into the soil, spacing them about 15cm apart. Garlic likes cold temperatures, and it actually needs several weeks below 10°C after planting if it is to produce lots of new cloves (if it doesn't get cold enough, you'll just get one clove). Keep away the weeds and water your garlic well, but don't let it sit in waterlogged soil.

You can grow garlic in containers if they are deep, and this is one way to ensure good drainage. I've had some success growing garlic in old chimney pots, placed directly on the soil and filled with organic compost and a little sand.

'Hardneck' garlic varieties produce a long, tender flower stalk called a scape ('softneck' varieties don't usually flower). The scape should be removed once it starts to curl round on itself and before the top starts to open, so the plant can direct all its energy into its bulb. Scapes are delicious lightly cooked.

The immature 'green garlic' bulbs can be harvested in spring or early summer when the leaves are still green. Mature garlic is ready to harvest in the summer once its leaves have turned yellow – usually July but later for spring-planted types. The garlic is ready to be used straight away or you can dry it, ideally just by leaving it outside for a few days in warm, sunny weather; it can then be stored for several months in a cool, dry, well-ventilated place.

Incidentally, garlic is an excellent companion plant for carrots as its scent helps to ward off carrot fly. It's also a traditional companion to roses because, according to legend, it is a sure-fire way to deter greenfly. Many anecdotal sources corroborate this, while the charming *Old Wives' Lore for Gardeners*, published in the 1970s, goes so far as to call garlic 'the systemic insecticide to end all others'.

# Horseradish *Armoracia rusticana*

| PLANT GROUP | Hardy perennial |
|---|---|
| HARVEST | From September of the first year onwards |

Either you love the hot thwack of horseradish or you don't. If, like me, you do, it's worth finding a good source. Many greengrocers and farm shops now sell fat lengths of this gnarled root, usually in the colder months of the year, and it keeps well, tightly wrapped, in the fridge. It's then ready to use – either in quantity as the main player in a sauce or dressing, or in smaller pinches as a fiery seasoning. This magnificently foliated plant is easy to cultivate and grows readily in the wild – swathes of plumey horseradish can be seen populating roadsides and waste ground all over the country. It is easily recognisable from its glossy leaves, which are like giant ruffled dock leaves. To be extra sure, crush some of the leaf between your fingers and you will get a faint whiff of that horseradish scent. You should know that digging up the root of any wild plant is illegal, unless you have the permission of the landowner. Personally, I imagine few landowners would begrudge you a root or two of this prolific weed, as long as you don't damage anything else.

## In the kitchen

When grated, horseradish releases pungent fumes which burn the nose and wet the eyes. As with chilli and pepper and mustard, that irritation and its accompanying endorphin high is fundamental to the delicious horseradish experience. The fumes (thiocyanites, if you want to know) are highly volatile, however, and soon lost. That's why freshly grated horseradish, mixed into an acidic stabilising medium, always tastes better than any that's been grated and stored. My basic preparation of horseradish is to peel a small section of root, grate it (I use a fine Microplane grater) and immediately combine it with enough lemon juice to make a damp (but not wet) mixture. You can also use vinegar to stabilise the grated root but I think lemon juice allows the horseradish flavour to shine a little more. Use straight away or keep, covered, in the fridge for a day or two.

- Blend a little freshly grated 'lemon-ed' horseradish root with crème fraîche and a pinch of sugar. Use this simple horseradish cream as a finishing touch to a soup – beetroot, carrot or pumpkin especially. It's also excellent as a dressing for, say, smoked mackerel and a heap of watercress.
- To make a dressing for coleslaw, add some grated horseradish to plain full-fat yoghurt, thin down with a little olive oil and season to taste. This is particularly nice with a mixture of shredded red cabbage and grated carrot.

- Stir some freshly grated horseradish root into softened unsalted butter with an extra squeeze of lemon juice, chopped parsley or chives and some seasoning. Use on baked or plain boiled potatoes.
- **Horseradish sauce** (p.161)

## How to grow

Horseradish is generally propagated from the root, not seed. You can either buy a young specimen or replant a section of root from a mature plant.

Spring is the ideal time to plant, but pretty much any bit of horseradish root, once put in the ground and given some water, will grow into a new plant. It's not fussy, but to maximise your chances of a long, strong root, give it moist, deep, rich soil and some sun. If you want to put it in a container, it needs to be a deep one.

The flavour becomes stronger as it grows and is really eye-watering around midwinter of its first year but you should be able to find useful amounts of root on a first-year plant from early autumn onwards.

Horseradish is an invasive plant. Pull up what you don't need or want – and be prepared to do this often, once it's taken hold. If there's a significant amount of root attached, so much the better – a great gift for a culinary friend.

# Hyssop *Hyssopus officinalis*

| PLANT GROUP | Hardy perennial |
|---|---|
| HARVEST | All year round |

This has become one of my favourite herbs. It's just so pretty in the garden, its narrow, dark green leaves complemented by either blue, white or pink flowers, to which you will often find a bee or two happily attached. The flavour comprises a sour, bitter lemonish tang over a deep rosemary-like resinousness. The result is quite bitter if you eat it neat, but this herb is incredibly delicious when mingled with creamy, rich or salty ingredients. Do not confuse it with anise hyssop (p.43), which is completely different.

## In the kitchen
Use hyssop almost as you would lemon juice or black pepper, as a seasoning and a foil to rich, unctuous foods. Add it fairly sparingly and experiment with eating it raw and cooked.

- I love hyssop with cheese. Scatter it whole or coarsely chopped over fried halloumi or a mozzarella salad.
- A sprinkling of hyssop used to finish a buttery, garlicky mushroom pasta dish cuts the richness very nicely.
- Add the chopped leaves to rich meaty stews and soups. The technique of adding some at the beginning of cooking and some at the end is worthwhile to get the full benefit of its complex flavour.
- Hyssop is a natural choice for homemade burgers, sausages or stuffings – try substituting it for sage in a sage and onion stuffing (p.129).
- **Baked white fish with a hyssop and orange crust (p.188)**

## How to grow
Hyssop is not difficult to grow from seed. It can be sown indoors from March, or straight into the ground in late spring. If you're impatient, like me, buy an established young plant. As a native of the Mediterranean, hyssop desires a sunny, well-drained location on light soil. Try it in a pot that can be moved to the garden's hottest spots or sited on a windowsill.

It should be cut back hard in the spring to promote new growth and the flowers deadheaded in the summer to encourage fresh leaves. When flowering, it's a good plant for bees. So far, mine has surprised me with its hardiness and vigour, still valiantly offering some snippets of leaf even in bitter winter weather.

# Lavender *Lavandula*

| | |
|---|---|
| **PLANT GROUP** | Hardy evergreen perennial (some varieties half-hardy) |
| **HARVEST** | May–July |

One of my earliest memories is of my grandmother showing me how to crush purple lavender flowerheads in my small fist to release their deep, warm scent. To this day, I can't pass a lavender bush without reaching out to grasp a stem or two, and the sight of this elegant silver-stemmed plant, nodding in the breeze, is not something I'd want to be without in my garden. That beautiful scent attracts bees and butterflies, while a few cut stems brought into the house in a jug or jam jar always look incredibly pretty. But lavender is a valuable culinary herb too, with a warm, aromatic and subtly floral flavour.

Like many herbs, lavender contains camphor among its aromatic compounds. Camphor is not a particularly pleasant flavour so, for cooking, you want a lavender with low levels. To ensure this, choose a *Lavandula angustifolia* variety and harvest the leaves and flower buds in the spring and early summer when the flavour is more delicate. *Angustifolia* have a more fragrant, sweeter taste than some of the alternative species, such as the bract-topped French lavender (*Lavandula stoechas*), which can be harsh. 'Hidcote' is a classic, hardy and very widely available cultivar of *Lavandula angustifolia*, and you can't really go wrong with it, but there are many others, such as 'Munstead' and 'Alba', which has white flowers.

There is an exception to the *angustifolia* rule: the hybrid *Lavandula* x *intermedia* 'Provence' is rated by some as the best of all for cooking. You will need to go to a specialist grower to find it (see Directory, p.248). For myself, I'd say it certainly gives very good results, but it doesn't put *angustifolia* in the shade.

## In the kitchen

Use lavender leaves for cooking, as well as flowers. Both can be dried but I always use fresh. Commercially dried flowers are available to use when lavender is out of season, but the flavour and scent are never as sweet and fragrant as fresh. Dried lavender is also pretty pungent, so halve the quantity. Ideally, cook with lavender during the spring and early summer, choosing tender leaves and flower buds which are developed and just tinged with colour, but not fully opened. I have used fresh lavender leaves well into the autumn, but the flavour is definitely a little less fine.

- Stir 1 tbsp chopped fresh lavender into a plain cake mixture. This is particularly nice used to make fairy cakes. Ice with a simple white glacé icing, then top with a few lavender buds, marigold petals or borage flowers.

Lavender *Lavandula angustifolia* 'Munstead'

- To make a lavender-scented syrup, put 150g caster sugar and 150ml water in a saucepan. Heat gently, stirring often, until the sugar has dissolved, then increase the heat. Add 1–2 tbsp fresh lavender buds and/or chopped leaves. Once simmering, cook gently for 5 minutes. Remove from the heat, cool and strain before using. This scented syrup is lovely with peaches, raspberries or strawberries, or try a delicate trickle on vanilla ice cream. It will keep in the fridge for at least a week.
- I love a little sprig of lavender combined with mint in a fresh herb tea.
- **Loin of lamb with lavender and lemon thyme** (p.194)
- **Lemon and lavender biscuits** (p.225)
- **Herb ice cream or custard** (p.219)
- **Apple herb jelly** (p.232)

## How to grow

There are many different species of lavender and they often do not 'come true' from seed, which means the new plant may not turn out to be the same as its parent. I would buy a young plant – ideally from a specialist grower (see Directory, p.248). You can also take cuttings from established lavenders (see p.34).

A native of the Mediterranean, lavender will thrive best in a sunny, open place, on light free-draining soil. Wet winters are bad news, as lavender tends not to do well in cold waterlogged soil. Making sure it is as well drained as possible is the best precaution, and digging sand or grit into your patch before planting is almost certainly a good idea unless you already have a very sandy soil. Lavender also grows well in a container.

To keep a lavender plant relatively neat and tidy, with plenty of new growth and not too much woodiness, it needs regular cutting. It's best to do this in spring and summer and if you're harvesting regularly, you'll effectively be trimming it anyway. Late in the summer, after flowering, give it a more wholesale cut-back, reducing the size of the plant by anything up to 50 per cent. Don't cut into the old wood and leave some green shoots on the plant, as it needs these to help it regenerate. You will find marvellous gnarled old lavender bushes in some gardens, their twisted woody stems bristling incongruously with the new year's green growth. But it's a good idea to replace the plant completely every 3–5 years, in order to give yourself plenty of fresh tender foliage and flowers.

# Lemon balm *Melissa officinalis*

| PLANT GROUP | Hardy perennial |
|---|---|
| HARVEST | April–September |

Also sometimes called melissa, this is one of the first herbs I ever grew and I always like to have some in the garden. It's such an easy, generous plant, sending up its gold-green leaves year after year, whether you tend it carefully or not, and offering a mild, sweet lemony flavour.

## In the kitchen

This is a gently flavoured creature – much more delicate than other lemony herbs, such as lemon thyme or lemon verbena. I turn to it most often to perfume and lift a cup of tea – either on its own or combined with black tea – but you can add it to dishes as well. Using the herb raw or infused is the way to go, rather than subjecting it to direct heat.

- You can use lemon balm raw in salads – fruit or vegetable – finely shredded for a delicious hint of lemony flavour. The young leaf tips make a beautiful edible garnish.
- Chop lemon balm leaves with other fairly delicate herbs such as parsley and fennel to make a light summery mix for an omelette, or to finish a soup.
- Try adding a generous quantity of finely chopped lemon balm leaves to a sponge cake batter.

## How to grow

Lemon balm grows easily and vigorously and is invasive. Plant it in a corner and, by next year, it will be coming up between your paving stones halfway across the garden. For this reason, it's a good herb to grow in a pot, but make it a large one, so the plant can stretch its legs and show off its lovely foliage.

You can start it from seed in plugs. Alternatively, dig up an established melissa in spring or autumn and divide the roots to form two or three new plants to be replanted. It doesn't need much except sun and water. Cut it regularly, removing flowerheads, to keep it bushy and lush through the summer. If you leave some flowers, however, it will attract plenty of bees. Lemon balm dies right back in winter but don't worry, it will return.

# Lemon verbena *Aloysia triphylla*

| PLANT GROUP | Half-hardy deciduous perennial |
| --- | --- |
| HARVEST | May–October |

With its elegant elongated leaves, lemon verbena looks rather demure but, in fact, it packs an intense punch of fragrant citrus flavour. What's more, though it's hard to believe when you first see a tender little verbena plant, it will eventually grow into a gorgeously scented, beautiful shrub – a lovely thing to have in your garden.

## In the kitchen
The flavour of this herb is incomparable: intensely lemony, floral, perfumed and slightly piney. The flavour comes predominantly from a compound called citral, which is also found in lemongrass. Lemon verbena is indeed a powerfully lemony ingredient, more pungent than lemon balm or lemon thyme and an absolute gift in sweet recipes. It also has savoury applications but do go gently with it – too much can actually make a dish taste rather synthetic. Always chop lemon verbena very finely if it's to be eaten, because the leaves are very slightly tough and waxy.

- Lemon verbena is a great flavouring for a custard or ice cream (see p.219).
- A verbena syrup, made in the same way as a lavender syrup (see p.89), is delicious trickled over cakes or fruit salads.
- For verbena sugar, pound 2–3 tbsp finely chopped young lemon verbena leaves with a roughly equivalent amount of golden caster sugar using a pestle and mortar until you have a fine, pale green sugar. Sprinkle over fruit or a cheesecake. Use the sugar up quickly as the flavour will fade.
- Lemon verbena makes a lovely tea – on its own or with mint (see p.244).
- **Lemon verbena layer with raspberries** (p.220)
- **Apple herb jelly** (p.232)

## How to grow
A young verbena plant will grow beautifully in a pot or, if you want to let it develop its full shrubby potential, plant it in the ground in a well-drained, sunny, sheltered place – against a south-facing wall would be ideal. In very cold weather it's a good idea to mulch it (put a thick insulating layer of compost, hay or other mulching material around the roots). If it's in a pot, you can bring it inside. It loses its leaves in winter but should come back with a vengeance in late spring or early summer. Cut it back in the autumn to encourage fresh bushy growth.

Lemon verbena is difficult to raise from seeds or cuttings in our climate.

# Lemongrass *Cymbopogon citrates*

| PLANT GROUP | Tender perennial |
|---|---|
| HARVEST | May–October |

Lemongrass is unlike any other herb – or, indeed, any other flavouring – in the sweet, pungent aromatic lift it contributes to a dish. We associate it primarily with the cooking of southeast Asia, and Thai curries in particular, but there's no reason not to exploit its perfumed lemonyness in other dishes, including soups and puddings. If you grow the herb yourself, you have the advantage of being able to use its long, slender leaves as well as its stem. The leaves are milder but share the same unique flavour and are great in a spicy soup or a tea.

## In the kitchen

Finely sliced or chopped lemongrass is fantastic in curry pastes, soups and dips and it is a great companion to chilli, lime, garlic, ginger, coriander and mint. Lemongrass has a lovely tender centre, but a very tough, fibrous outer layer. To get nicely chopped lemongrass that won't stick in your teeth, you have to peel off at least three outer layers of the stem. These are too fibrous to eat, but you can add them to a soup, stock or syrup to infuse with a lemongrass flavour. Once you've got down to the heart of the stem, where it feels tender and easily sliceable, start chopping. Sometimes the yield from one stem is not very great and that's why I often use two stems when a recipe calls for one. Lemongrass stems freeze well.

- Lemongrass is a key ingredient – typically pounded with garlic, chillies, lime, ginger and coriander – in Thai curry pastes and laksa soups.
- Infusing a bashed lemongrass stem in a syrup (as for lavender syrup, see p.89) makes a fragrant drizzle for cakes or puddings, or a base for a sorbet.
- Immerse a bruised lemongrass stem in the liquid when poaching fruit such as pears.
- Try adding a bashed stem of lemongrass to rice while it's cooking.
- For a slightly more subtle flavour than you get with chopped lemongrass, you can put a whole stem, just lightly bruised to help release the flavour, into a simmering soup or curry.
- Lemongrass is great with fish. Try it in a marinade for scallops, or in crab or fish cakes.
- You can infuse lemongrass in drinks – use in herbal teas (see p.244) or in a scented lemonade (p.241).
- **Herb noodle soup (p.173)**

## How to grow

Lemongrass is well worth growing because you can then exploit the leaves as well as the stem (you only get the stem if you buy it in the shops). It can be grown from seed in spring (it needs lots of warmth and takes some time to germinate – up to a month), or bought as a young plant.

However, you should be able to get a shop-bought cut stem to take root as well. Make sure there is a bit of woody base still on the stem then put it in a glass of water. Within a few weeks, it should have formed a ball of roots (see below). Plant it in a pot, keep it moist and warm and it will start to produce green leaves and new stems. Lemongrass eventually develops into a flamboyant multi-stemmed plant with a great crown of grassy leaves.

Unless you live somewhere near the Equator, this herb is best kept in a pot. It needs warmth – don't let it get below 7°C – and moisture during the spring to autumn growing season. Although lemongrass should be all right outside in high summer, growing it indoors, or in a warm greenhouse, is probably the best plan.

You can harvest both the leaves and the whole lemongrass stems, cutting them off at the base. In winter, the plant needs little water, but still plenty of warmth, and it should regenerate in spring. You can divide established clumps to create new plants.

Rooting lemongrass stems

Slicing peeled lemongrass stems

# Lovage *Levisticum officinale*

| PLANT GROUP | Hardy perennial |
|---|---|
| HARVEST | April–September |

I love lovage and I am not alone: I know several herb-growers and cooks who rate it as one of their favourite herbs. It has the most amazing powerful, deeply savoury scent and flavour – akin to celery but more intense, more spicy, more complex. Its unique backnote can add great depth and strength to soups or stocks, and I also love it combined with eggs and cheese.

You can now buy lovage in some supermarkets as well as from more adventurous greengrocers' and farm shops. However, it's not as widely available as, say, parsley, rosemary and thyme, so you've everything to gain by raising your own. To that I must add that lovage is a vigorous grower. Over the period of a few years, it can reach over 2 metres in height and 1 metre in width, dwarfing other herbs and, indeed, you. So give it some space but enjoy its stature. You'll rarely need more than a few leaves of lovage at a time, so you can rely on even a smaller plant to provide structure and presence in your herb patch throughout the year.

## In the kitchen

Lovage is often written about with a hint of warning – it certainly is very strong, and it will leave its tenacious scent on your fingers long after you've picked it. But it is a herb to be embraced, not feared. The key is to choose the younger, more tender leaves, and to use it in small amounts. Literally a couple of leaves or two added to a stock will give it weight and character, and a teaspoonful or two of chopped lovage stirred into a soup at the beginning of cooking lends an amazing depth – added at the end, it is akin to a spice.

- Very young, mild lovage leaves can be added straight to a salad.
- Finely chopped lovage adds a great flavour to a homemade burger mix.
- Wrap a wedge of Cheddar, Wensleydale or other firm, nutty cheese in a few lovage leaves, securing the package in greaseproof paper or cling film. After a few days the flavour will have subtly and deliciously permeated.
- Chopped lovage added to wilted greens, such as spinach or rocket, gives them body and richness.
- A whisper of lovage stirred into the beaten egg for an omelette or frittata is very good, especially when combined with waxy new potatoes.
- Another nice way to use lovage very subtly is to crush a few leaves and rub them around a bowl before pouring in almost any kind of veg-based soup.

- Lovage is good with parsley – use much more parsley than lovage. I really like this herb duo in an omelette (see p.182), or stirred into freshly cooked rice with sautéed onion and toasted pine nuts to make a simple sort of pilaf.
- Try finely chopped lovage in a cheese sandwich, or with cheese on toast.
- **Celery leaf and lovage soup** (p.172)
- **Beef stew with lovage** (p.192)

## How to grow

You can sow lovage seeds in plugs – or directly into the garden – in the spring or summer. You can also dig up the roots of existing plants in spring, cut off pieces of root with growing shoots attached and replant these. Lovage is not overly fussy but prefers a sunny position on rich soil. Give it plenty of space as it grows quickly and expansively. You can also contain it in a reasonably sized pot.

The older the leaves, the more intense, even overpowering, the flavour. Therefore, for the cook, it's a good idea to cut the plant right back in the summer, in order to encourage new tender growth. Allow lovage to die back in the winter and it will start to send up shoots early in the spring.

Wrapping cheese in lovage leaves

# Marigold *Calendula officinalis*

| PLANT GROUP | Hardy annual |
|---|---|
| HARVEST | May–October |

These pretty flowers are the bustling cherry-cheeked housewives of the herb garden. All good will and enthusiasm, they bring sunshine to any border or patch, offer one of the simplest and prettiest of all herb garnishes, and are hard-working companion plants to boot (see below). The name, so it goes, is a contraction of 'Mary's gold', an epithet that honours the Virgin.

You can eat both the leaves and the petals of the marigold. There's not much discernible flavour in the petals. They're pleasant enough to eat, with a delicate, sweet nuttiness when cooked, but, for me, they're all about the vibrant colour, and that's reason enough to add them to a dish. The young leaves, on the other hand, have a lovely taste – fresh and sweetish, with a peppery finish.

## In the kitchen

Fresh marigold petals are just gorgeous as a garnish. Many sources will tell you that you can also infuse the petals in liquid or fat and use the golden colour to stain other foodstuffs – a sort of poor man's saffron, though without the pungent flavour. I have tried warming them in water, milk, butter and oil and can report zero success with this enterprise (although, lightly fried, they taste lovely). My petals stubbornly hang on to their colour.

- Pluck marigold petals from a freshly picked flowerhead and scatter them directly on to salads, cakes, fruity puddings – even pizzas or tarts, dips or summery soups.
- The leaves are very good in salads – go for the young, slender, tender ones.
- **Green and gold salad** (p.176)

## How to grow

This is a very low-maintenance herb. Marigolds grow easily and prolifically and, though they are annuals, they will self-seed without encouragement. You can sow your own seed, of course – scattering it straight into a patch of well-drained soil in the spring. Marigolds like to soak up the sun, but aren't too fussy beyond that. Remove dead heads to prolong flowering (if you have a decent clump of marigolds, this will become an almost daily task by late summer). They make nice pot plants.

Marigolds are often used as companion plants – they deter asparagus beetle and attract predators such as hoverflies, which eat aphids. They are also attractive to blackfly, luring them away from other plants. This is unfortunate, of course, if it's the marigolds you want to use. The trick is to get rid of the blackfly before they take hold because as soon as a few take up residence they send out 'come on over, the party's started' signals to all their friends and relations. On hot, humid days, check your marigolds assiduously. Remove any blackfly you find by simply wiping them off. You can also cut away the affected part of the plant if it isn't too large. If the flies really are building up, you can spray the affected parts with a solution of horticultural soft soap (see Directory, p.249); this is not the same as detergent. The herb will still be safe to eat within a few days, as long as you wash it well first.

## Relatives

*Calendula officinalis* is also widely known as pot marigold or common marigold. *Tagetes patula*, or French marigold, is a different species. It is not good to eat, but is prized as a companion plant, emitting a strong scent as well as a substance from the roots that deters unwelcome soil-bound creatures including nematodes and slugs. French marigolds are particularly valuable alongside potatoes and tomatoes but many gardeners rate them as one of the best all-round companions in the veg patch.

Marigold *Calendula officinalis*

Marjoram *Origanum majorana*

# Marjoram and oregano

*Origanum majorana; Origanum vulgare*

| PLANT GROUP | Half-hardy perennial; hardy perennial |
| --- | --- |
| HARVEST | May–October |

What is the difference between marjoram and oregano? It's a question of intensity, really. Both are members of the *Origanum* genus and share similar warm, spicy flavour characteristics, but they are different species. If you buy a fresh herb labelled 'marjoram', it is likely to be *Origanum majorana*, or sweet marjoram, whereas something called 'oregano' is more likely to be *Origanum vulgare*, also called pot marjoram or wild marjoram. The former has a finer, sweeter flavour; the latter is more pungent and earthy.

Generally, marjoram is considered culinarily superior and would perhaps be the one to choose if you wanted to grow just one *Origanum* species. It's also the case that the flavour of oregano can vary a lot depending on the climate and its situation. When grown in hot, dry places, it tends to be much more intense and flavourful, hence its importance in both Mediterranean and South American cooking.

## In the kitchen

Think of these as two siblings. The more tender and delicate marjoram needs a little mollycoddling and is best used raw or briefly cooked, with lighter flavours such as raw tomatoes, green vegetables, cheese, chicken or fish. Big, tough oregano can look after itself, so chuck it whole or chopped into a chilli, stews, soups and slow-cooked tomato sauces.

Oregano is one of the few herbs that dries really well and a good-quality bought version can be useful (and in some cases better than the fresh herb) for hearty winter cooking with tinned tomatoes, dried beans or red meat.

- For a lovely supper dish, try spaghetti squash with marjoram. Fry a sliced garlic clove extremely gently in 2 tbsp olive or rapeseed oil for a couple of minutes. Add the broken-up flesh of a cooked spaghetti squash (or any cooked squash or pumpkin for that matter) and toss in the oil to reheat. Stir in a knob of butter, a generous tbsp chopped marjoram and plenty of salt and pepper. Serve as it is, or tossed into pasta, with lots of finely grated Parmesan sprinkled on top.
- Try these herbs roughly chopped in any tomato sauce. Add oregano at the beginning of cooking and marjoram at the end – or do both!

- Scrunch a few marjoram or oregano leaves in your fingers and rub them into the surface of some just-toasted sourdough bread. Trickle with oil and sprinkle with salt and you have a fantastic bruschetta to be eaten just as it is or topped with raw tomatoes and slivers of Parmesan.
- Baby leaves of marjoram are fantastic sprinkled on a just-baked pizza.
- Oregano takes baked mushrooms to a whole new level. Choose big open-capped mushrooms, place stalk side up in an oven dish and scatter with chopped garlic, salt and pepper and lots of the finely chopped herb. Add a little knob of butter to each mushroom. Bake at 190°C/Gas mark 5 for 15–20 minutes until tender, juicy and bubbling. Serve as a starter or a side dish. These mushrooms are very nice simply with a jacket potato and a green salad.
- **Salmoriglio sauce** (p.165)
- **Herb omelette** (p.182)

## How to grow

I always tend to buy the woodier perennial herbs like these as young plants, so that the work of getting them established has already been done, but you can grow them from seed if you want to. Oregano (*Origanum vulgare*) can be sown in plugs at any time, but marjoram (*Origanum majorana*) should be sown in early spring; both need warmth to germinate. Once established, *origanum* species like sunshine and dry conditions. Marjoram is only half-hardy and is often grown as an annual, even though it is technically a perennial. It likes a chalky soil. Oregano is a tougher customer and more likely to thrive year after year as long as it's grown in a sheltered, sunny, well-drained spot. Both are good grown in pots. They should be cut back after flowering and again in the autumn.

## Relatives

Greek oregano (*Origanum vulgare* subsp. *hirtum* 'Greek') is very intense and pungent and an inimitable part of Greek cooking, though it may be hard to get it to realise its true flavour potential in our climate.

There are many other varieties of *Origanum* to choose from, including golden and variegated ones, many of which are very pretty. All are worth experimenting with but it is still probably good old *Origanum majorana* that will give you the greatest culinary satisfaction. I have found the flavour of the variegated 'Gold Tip' variety particularly disappointing.

Oregano *Origanum vulgare*

Spearmint *Mentha spicata*

# Mint *Mentha*

| PLANT GROUP | Hardy perennial |
|---|---|
| HARVEST | April–October |

The clean, refreshing sweetness of mint is welcome in a multitude of dishes, sweet and savoury, making this surely one of the most useful of all culinary herbs. It's an easy herb to buy, but the quality can be hit and miss. You may well get a lovely aromatic bunch of leaves from a supermarket or greengrocer, but sometimes it will be disappointing. I like to grow mint (it's ridiculously easy to do) so a cup of mint tea, a pepped-up fruit salad or even a summery mint pesto are never far away.

There are numerous different types of mint, but the three main species are spearmint (*Mentha spicata*), peppermint (*Mentha* x *piperita*) and applemint (*Mentha suaveolens*). As a general rule, spearmint is sweeter, peppermint is sharper, fresher, more pungent and mentholly, and applemint is milder and more subtle.

Spearmint, also known as garden mint, is the best all-rounder and is what you'll get if you buy mint from a supermarket. If you grow your own, two varieties, Moroccan mint (*Mentha spicata crispa* 'Moroccan') and Tashkent mint (*Mentha spicata* 'Tashkent'), are particularly good for fresh mint tea (see p.244). However, there are those who swear that only a peppermint such as black peppermint (*Mentha* x *piperita* 'Black Peppermint') should be used for infusions.

Peppermints can be useful for cooking too, particularly in syrups or puddings where you want quite a penetrating mint flavour. *Mentha* x *piperita* 'Berries and Cream' is lovely in a fruit salad. If you're looking to grow your own mint, and you only have space for one, I'd try Moroccan mint. But if you can get some peppermint in too, even better. Applemint, with its furry leaves, is worth growing but will tend to lose its flavour when exposed to heat, so try it chopped raw into salads.

## In the kitchen

Mint is delicious in so many things, just use it as fresh as possible. Although it will give up its flavour beautifully when infused in a hot liquid, you shouldn't actually cook it for any length of time. It's also worth investigating dried mint – a traditional ingredient in many Greek, Turkish and Arabic dishes. It adds an authentic, strong and, I think, almost smoky tea-like flavour to kebabs, stuffings, salads and soups.

- You'll know that adding a stem of fresh spearmint to simmering peas or new potatoes enhances their flavour beautifully. But you can do the same with almost any vegetable, as well as lentils and beans. Adding finely chopped mint and a knob of butter to the cooked veg takes things a step further.

- For a tabbouleh salad, mix cooked bulgar wheat (or couscous, pearled spelt or barley) with a vast quantity of finely chopped parsley and a slightly less vast quantity of spearmint. Add diced tomatoes, the very best olive oil you can afford, a spritz of lemon juice and plenty of salt and pepper.
- Shredded or roughly chopped mint is a good addition to a fruit salad. It's particularly complementary to strawberries and I also love it with mango.
- If you want to experiment with dried mint, try this simple dip/sauce. Whisk together 3 tbsp plain yoghurt, 1 tbsp olive oil, 1 tsp dried mint, a pinch of dried chilli flakes, a scrap of crushed garlic and some salt and pepper. Leave for at least 30 minutes for the flavours to develop, then serve with falafel, or as a sauce for kebabs or chicken, stuffed into pita breads.
- **Mint sauce** (p.163)
- **Minty chocolate fridge cake** (p.226)
- **Minty apple mojito** (p.243)
- **Minted red berry sorbet** (p.216)
- **Apple herb jelly** (p.232)

## How to grow

Mint is rarely grown from seed, as there are no guarantees of exactly what you'll get. But plants are very easy to grow – your problem is more likely to be how to stop them. Mints like plenty of water, a rich soil and partial or full sun but, even in less than perfect conditions, these are rampant and invasive growers. They are best planted in large containers (I use an old half-barrel). If planting directly into a bed, limit spread by planting your mint within a large bucket or similar container with the bottom cut out, sunk into the soil.

Keep different varieties separate as they can cross-pollinate. Water them well and feed the soil (see p.36) a few times during the growing season. Cut back to the ground in winter, feed the soil with compost or manure and your mint should flourish again the following year. It's worth replacing plants every few years.

It's easy to propagate new from old. Just dig up a section of root and cut a piece which has a young growing shoot attached. Plant this and it will soon establish a new plant. Remove any flowering stems to keep the plant bushy and tender.

## Relatives

Of the many varieties, special mention must go to two other much-loved species at River Cottage. Eastern mint (*Mentha longifolia* subsp. *schimperi*) doesn't look like a mint at all, with its long, pointed silvery leaves. It is very strong and pepperminty, and good in tea. Then there is Kentucky mint (*Mentha spicata* 'Kentucky Colonel'), a very sweet, fragrant herb, which is traditionally used in a mint julep cocktail but works equally well in other drinks, such as a mojito (p.243).

Peppermint *Mentha* x *piperita* 'Berries and Cream'

# Myrtle *Myrtus communis*

| PLANT GROUP | Half-hardy evergreen shrub |
|---|---|
| HARVEST | All year round |

This slightly waxy-leaved herb is beautifully aromatic. Crush some leaves, take a sniff and you will find a sweet, almost orangey note which gives way to a fragrance reminiscent of both bay and juniper. The flavour has a bitter, astringent edge too. Myrtle has leaves all year round, so it's an ideal winter ingredient. It also produces berries which you can use as an alternative to juniper. In parts of the Mediterranean, branches of myrtle are traditionally thrown on cooking fires to flavour food, and you can put trimmings from the plant over barbecue coals to the same end.

Do not confuse this herb with lemon myrtle, which is a different thing altogether (an Australian tree with intensely lemony and aromatic leaves).

## In the kitchen

You can use fresh myrtle leaves almost like miniature bay leaves, though the flavour is more subtle and more fugitive, so add towards the end of cooking. The leaves work well chopped or crushed too, and combined with other herbs or added to stews. The herb has a slight bitterness so err on the side of caution when using it.

- Stuff myrtle leaves into the cavity of a fish before baking, then press some more into slashes cut in the sides of the fish. You can also stuff the leaves into the cavity of a chicken or any game bird before roasting.
- Add a few chopped leaves to a beef or game stew at the end of cooking.
- The dried berries can be used in a similar way to juniper berries – lightly crushed and added to marinades for red meat.
- **Roast chicken with lemon and myrtle** (p.198)

## How to grow

You have to be a little bit careful with myrtle. It really doesn't like to get too wet or too cold. Buy it as a young shrub and choose its position with care – a sheltered, sunny place is essential and free-draining soil. It can be finished off by winter rain or by heavy frost – if this is forecast, you can protect it with horticultural fleece.

Myrtle is a good herb to grow in a pot, so you can move it when necessary – though it can grow up to 3 metres given the chance.

## Relatives

*Myrtus communis* subsp. *tarentina* is a particularly pretty small-leaved variety.

# Nasturtium *Tropaeolum majus*

| PLANT GROUP | Half-hardy annual |
| --- | --- |
| HARVEST | May–August |

These are such wonderful edible plants, offering both stunning flowers that look fantastic in salads and intensely peppery green leaves to rival rocket or mizuna. You can even harvest and pickle the peppery little seed pods and eat them like capers, as Pam Corbin describes in her *River Cottage Preserves Handbook*. You can buy nasturtiums as a summer ingredient from some enterprising outlets, but they don't travel well and this is an easy plant to grow in a pot on a patio.

## In the kitchen

Nasturtium leaves are very spicy and best used when young and tender, combined with something else. The flowers are a little sweeter and milder, but still peppery.

- Add the flowers at the last minute to a light salad of dressed lettuce, or scatter over more substantial salads – potato or cucumber or fennel, say.
- Toss young nasturtium leaves, shredded or torn, with sweeter salad leaves.
- You can also wilt the leaves down in a soup or even toss into a pasta dish.
- To make nasturtium leaf mayonnaise, stir 1 tbsp finely chopped nasturtium leaves (around 6 leaves) into about 150ml mayonnaise (p.159). This is great in chicken sandwiches or with cold fish.
- **Nasturtium flower dressing** (p.164)

## How to grow

Nasturtiums are easy to raise from seed, in plugs or sown direct into the ground in spring. They are also sold as young plants by the trayful. Plant them in full sun – they're happy in most conditions but prefer a poor soil – and keep them well watered. They're a great choice for pots or hanging baskets, but also look lovely around the edges of a herb garden. Remove the dead heads as soon as the flowers wilt, but look out for the seed pods if you want to collect them.

There are lots of different nasturtium varieties to choose from, with all sorts of glorious colours, but I do not believe you will notice any great difference between them in terms of flavour.

The one drawback with growing nasturtiums is their tendency to attract blackfly. This makes them useful as companion plants, as they draw the little blighters away from your broad beans and cabbages, but it's pretty annoying if it's the nasturtiums themselves you want to eat. See my note on blackfly and marigolds (p.98).

Flat-leaf parsley *Petroselinum crispum* var. *neapolitana*

# Parsley, curly and flat-leaf

*Petroselinum crispum*; *P. crispum* var. *neapolitana*

| PLANT GROUP | Hardy biennials |
| --- | --- |
| HARVEST | All year round |

Ubiquitous and yet underrated, there's something of a paradox around parsley. It is so often used as the worst kind of garnish – one completely divorced from the dish it decorates and often uneatable. If it's not in the dish itself and you're not even going to eat it, what's the point? Parsley certainly can finish a dish beautifully, but it's much better added in such a way that it echoes or enhances the flavours, and can be consumed too. The fact is, though, this herb can be so much more than a finishing touch. It is a mild but aromatic and delicious leaf that should be used generously and broadly, one that subtly enhances everything from eggs and cheese to almost any kind of vegetable, via meat, fish and pulses. It rarely dominates a dish but pretty much always helps to define and deepen it.

## In the kitchen

Flat-leaf, also known as French or Italian parsley, has a fuller, finer flavour than curly. It's the one I instinctively turn to most often, and it is far nicer to eat raw. In fact, when whole or only roughly chopped, the leaves are fantastic used in quantity in salads, or even cooked as a vegetable. I have no issue with using coarser-textured, slightly less characterful curly parsley, as long as it is well chopped. In either case, I always think of parsley as a 'cool' herb, whose subtle, grassy, clean character balances richer, sweeter flavours beautifully.

- Parsley goes brilliantly with garlic, and also lemon. Gremolata, a mix of finely chopped garlic, parsley and lemon zest, is one of my favourite finishing touches (see p.80). Leave out the lemon for a persillade – an equally handy mix that transforms simple things such as fried potatoes or lamb chops when added to the pan at the very last minute.
- Whole leaves of flat-leaf parsley combined with cold cooked white beans or Puy lentils make a fantastic salad. Dress with a vinaigrette and add something a little sharp, such as finely chopped shallot or spring onion. Tomatoes are another good addition.
- Combine chopped parsley with tarragon, chives and chervil to create the classic blend *fines herbes*, which is extremely good in omelettes (see p.182) and other egg dishes.

- Use the coarse stalks of parsley in bouquets garnis, or add to stocks.
- Flat-leaf parsley can be used as a cooked vegetable too. Use at least 50g per person and remove all but the finest stems. You can either steam it until wilted then roughly chop, or chop it first then heat a generous knob of butter with a splash of oil in a large frying pan over a medium heat and cook the parsley until dark, wilted and reduced. In either case, season with salt, pepper and a squeeze of lemon. Serve as an intensely flavoured side dish, or use to top bruschetta.
- The fresh, grassy taste of parsley is lovely with root vegetables, particularly the sweeter ones like carrots, parsnips or celeriac. Any soup, purée or salad of any of these roots is enhanced by parsley.
- You can make a very good parsley sauce by simply stirring lots of finely chopped parsley into a bay-and-onion-infused béchamel sauce. This is especially good with baked gammon.
- **Basil and parsley pesto** (p.166)

## How to grow

This is a herb that's definitely worth growing, especially if you use as much of it as I do. The leaves you pick from the parsley plant in your backyard will be the freshest-tasting, most flavourful you'll ever eat. It isn't that I grow so much that I never need to buy any, but the just-picked stuff really is superb. Even a couple of good plants in a pot will provide you with abundant cutting leaves for salads. But if you put aside a good amount of space and sow your own two or three times during the year, you'll have a very decent crop.

Both types of parsley need plenty of warmth and moisture to germinate, so are best started inside. Germination is always slow. You can sow some in late summer and you should have parsley through the winter, though it may need protection with a cloche, cold frame or fleece if it's outside.

Parsley needs rich, moist soil and a mostly sunny position; you really shouldn't let the soil dry out. It also grows well in containers. As a biennial, parsley will naturally produce flowers and seeds and lose leaf quality in its second year, hence it is usually grown as an annual. Being part of the carrot family, it can attract carrot fly and it's worth planting it near onions or garlic to deter this pest.

Curly parsley *Petroselinum crispum*

Purple perilla *Perilla frutescens* var. *purpurascens*

# Perilla *Perilla frutescens*

| PLANT GROUP | Half-hardy annual |
| --- | --- |
| HARVEST | May–October |

This is a 'new' herb, i.e. one not traditional in our culinary culture, but it deserves to become an old favourite. You can get green and purple varieties. I have grown the latter and loved it – its magnificent jagged purple leaves immediately draw the eye. The flavour of perilla is unique and very interesting – sweetly pungent with a distinct note of cumin.

Also known as shiso, perilla is a herb most associated with Chinese and Japanese cooking. The green variety is typically served with sushi and sashimi, as a garnish for tempura, or used in stir-fries. Purple perilla is a classic ingredient in pickled umeboshi plums.

## In the kitchen

Perilla is related to basil and mint and can be used in similar ways. Green perilla has a particularly good flavour, whereas the purple variety looks fabulous. Neither variety will take well to long cooking. Instead, use the leaves raw or just wilted briefly, in generous quantities.

- Scatter shredded perilla on to noodle soups (see p.173).
- Add shredded to salads or wilt into fried vegetables.
- For a quick and delicious perilla prawn stir-fry, heat some sunflower oil in a wok over a high heat. Fry some thin strips of red pepper for a couple of minutes, then add some finely chopped garlic and chilli and fry for 30 seconds more. Throw in some peeled Atlantic prawns and stir-fry for a couple of minutes until cooked. Add 2–3 tbsp shredded perilla leaves and turn off the heat. Stir briefly until the perilla is wilted, season with salt and pepper and serve with rice or noodles.
- **Aubergines with perilla** (p.201)

## How to grow

This annual herb likes sun or partial shade and rich soil. Sow it indoors in spring, or outside in early summer. Alternatively, buy young plants and site them in a reasonably sheltered, sunny spot, or put them in pots. Once the plants are established, pinching out the growing tips encourages lots of bushy leafy growth. If you keep attending to it, you should have plenty of leaves through to autumn and, with luck, it will self-seed.

# Rocket, salad and wild

*Eruca vesicaria* subsp. *sativa*; *Diplotaxis muralis*

| PLANT GROUP | Half-hardy annual; hardy perennial |
|---|---|
| HARVEST | All year round |

Rocket, also known as roquette or arugula, has suffered from its own popularity. Now that it is so prevalent on menus and in supermarket salad bags, it's hardly the prized leaf it once was but forget that. It's a completely delicious and riotously peppery leaf that works equally well in small quantities as a herb or salad ingredient, or as the main player in a dish. There are two basic varieties: 'salad' rocket and the sharper-leaved, hotter-flavoured 'wild' rocket.

## In the kitchen

Rocket is, undoubtedly, a fantastic salad ingredient. In a green salad to be served up as a dish in its own right, I think this peppery leaf is best combined with other leaves that offer varying tastes and textures – some crisp cos and lemony sorrel, perhaps, or a few soft, sweet butterhead lettuce leaves and some chervil or parsley. However, when rocket is accompanying something else – like a big, hearty warm salad of roasted squash and walnuts, or a garlicky aubergine parmigiana or moussaka – it needs no amelioration. In most cases, I lean towards wild rocket rather than salad rocket, simply because the flavour is hotter and richer, and the leaf more elegantly spear-like. Your own tastes may take you in the other direction.

- Rocket can be wilted down in a little oil and/or butter in the same way as spinach (and is considerably less watery). Just pop it straight into the pan on a medium-low heat and cook until it collapses. I love it cooked like this and combined with sautéed fennel or raw tomatoes and tossed into pasta.
- Wilted with a little garlic, then chopped and combined with soft goat's cheese and a touch of grated Parmesan, rocket makes a delicious filling for homemade ravioli.
- Rocket is a superb partner to bland, rich, creamy ingredients like avocado and mozzarella, to salty-sharp things such as air-dried ham or capers, and to bulky starches like potatoes, squashes or pulses. Keep these attributes in mind and you can see that the salad possibilities are endless. Try, for instance, a few curls of peppery wild rocket with sliced cold potatoes and a good trickle of extra virgin olive oil. Add some shreds of air-dried ham and finish off with a few rocket flowers.

- Add rocket to soups, instead of or as well as spinach leaves.
- Scatter rocket leaves over an omelette before folding (see p.182).
- Both types of rocket produce small, pretty flowers, which are very good to eat too. They are particularly delicious sprinkled on a pizza before serving.

## How to grow

Rocket is easy to grow and if you sow your own every month or two from February to September you can create an almost year-round supply of fresh young leaves.

In early spring, start rocket seeds off in plugs. During warmer weather, choose a partly shaded spot and sow directly into the ground or a big pot. Cut the leaves as soon as they look big enough, as and when you want them, and the plants will grow more. After 2 or 3 months, the leaves will start to become tougher and more bitter and those plants can be pulled up and discarded.

In cold weather, salad rocket may need protection under a cold frame, cloche or fleece – or you can grow it in the greenhouse if you have one. Keep well watered in dry weather and cut the leaves often. Generally, the bigger and more mature rocket leaves are, the more peppery kick they have. Hot, dry conditions make the leaves more pungent too. Salad rocket has a tendency to bolt very quickly, especially in hot and dry weather, so is best for early spring or autumn sowing.

Wild rocket *Diplotaxis muralis*

Salad rocket *Eruca vesicaria sativa*

Climbing patio rose 'Nice Day'

# Rose *Rosa*

| | |
|---|---|
| **PLANT GROUP** | Perennial |
| **HARVEST** | June–July |

The scent and flavour of roses is not to everyone's taste but don't be put off the idea of using them in your cooking just because you don't like Turkish delight. Rose petals can be used to add flavour and scent in a very subtle way and a homemade infusion or preserve will be considerably less overpowering than many commercially prepared rose waters.

Roses for use in cooking or preserving must be deeply, headily fragranced. There is a huge and frankly fairly confusing variety to choose from. I selected two hybrid tea roses: deep red 'Velvet Fragrance' and the peachy 'Chandos Beauty', simply because of their exquisite perfume. Also recommended for their fragrance are 'Falstaff' and 'Munstead Wood' (both 'English' roses) and various types of Damask rose (*Rosa damascena*) and Apothecary's rose (*Rosa gallica*). *Rosa rugosa* is another useful species – a fast-growing, low-maintenance rose with a wonderful heavy scent. When buying roses, it's worth thinking about hardiness and disease resistance as well as perfume. Some types of rose, particularly *gallica* and *rugosa* roses, tick both boxes.

The best thing, undoubtedly, is to go to a specialist rose retailer, ask their advice and then have a good sniff around. A deep colour in the petals is important if you want your rose infusion to be a pretty pink. A mixture of petals that includes just a few deep red ones should be enough to give an enticing rose shade, but pale blooms can still give exquisite scent even with a less exotic colour. My first batch of rose petal jelly, made from peach-hued roses, turned out a beautiful deep honey shade.

It's important that the roses you use for any culinary purposes are unsprayed. Finding an organic grower of roses is nigh-on impossible and, although modern varieties are generally far more disease-resistant than many older ones, I think it's safe to assume that roses bought from any conventional retailer will almost certainly have been dosed with something. If you buy a rose in flower, wait for its original blooms to fade, then start harvesting the fresh unsprayed ones as they open. Alternatively, depending on when you buy your rose, you may have to wait until next year.

## In the kitchen

To capture the fragrance of rose petals, you need a good number of them and you need to infuse them in hot liquid. Once heated, they will wilt into an unprepossessing brownish tangle, but do not worry – their magical perfume will pass from their collapsed cells into the surrounding solution. Strain them from their hot bath and press the spent petals hard with a wooden spoon to extract every last drop of flavour.

- Perfect rose petals make a lovely garnish on a cake or cream-topped trifle. You can use them just as they are or frost them by brushing them delicately with lightly beaten egg white, then dusting with caster sugar. Don't expect too much in the way of flavour though – petals eaten neat like this may not taste of much at all. The white 'heel', where the petal joins the plant, can be bitter.
- **Rose petal jelly** (p.234)
- **Rose elixir** (p.241), ideal for adding to drinks

## How to grow

There is abundant specialist advice to be had about rose-growing and you should get good information from the grower you buy from. However, I think if you start off by looking at your rose bushes as being part of a lovely and varied herb garden, rather than as single specimens to be isolated and obsessed about, you are on the right track. Mixed planting and companion planting are at the heart of organic gardening and apply to roses as much as any other genus. This approach is one of the best ways to protect against disease.

Choose a well-drained sunny patch for your newly acquired rose plants and enrich the soil before planting with manure or compost. Early in the spring, prune them back hard. (The degree and style of pruning required depends on the type of rose, so ask when you buy.) Water roses in dry weather and be vigilant about watering if your roses are in containers. Feed them after pruning and again in the summer after their first flowering. Organic rose feeds and fertilisers are available. Deadhead regularly to encourage fresh flowers, cutting away old blooms cleanly with secateurs just above the next five-leafed stem.

Put in place a plan of defence against pests such as greenfly, with companion planting as the main plank of it. Good companion plants include garlic and other alliums that deter the dreaded aphids, and plants which attract hoverflies and insects that love to eat aphids – members of the Umbelliferae family, such as dill and fennel, as well as poppies, evening primroses and yarrow. If greenfly do appear, you can remove them by hand, though obviously this becomes an impossible task if your buds are really infested.

The fungus and moulds that sometimes attack roses are often a consequence of particular conditions – too much or too little rain, for instance. Concentrating on raising the healthiest plants you can – with an approach of mixed planting plus good pruning, watering and feeding – is the best precaution.

Rose *Rosa rugosa*

# Rosemary *Rosmarinus officinalis*

| PLANT GROUP | Hardy evergreen perennial |
|---|---|
| HARVEST | All year round |

Rosemary, as Ophelia said, is for remembrance, and this surely is one of the most evocatively scented herbs of all. I defy anyone to take a good breath of it and not be transported to a very lovely place. Viewed by aromatherapists as stimulating and mind-clearing, the scent of rosemary is also warming, penetrating and, to my mind, healing. Burning cuttings of the herb – either on a barbecue or open fire – is one lovely way to release its scent.

Rosemary is a pretty vital culinary herb. Its warm, resinous, piney scent is enticing and the flavour more than fulfils that promise. Like bay, it is enormously versatile and complements a huge range of foods. Also like bay, it has such a powerful character that you don't need to actually eat it to get the benefit – simply infusing it in a liquid, or cooking it alongside other ingredients, can be enough.

## In the kitchen

There are two basic ways to cook this herb. Firstly, as an infuser, whole sprigs can be tossed with roasting vegetables or immersed in a simmering stew or lightly crushed and added to a marinade. Secondly, you can use the flavour more directly by chopping the herb and adding it to a dish before or during cooking. The first method is obviously a little more subtle, but none the less effective. Take care with raw rosemary, as the leaves are relatively tough and there is a hint of bitterness to the herb, which is most noticeable when it is uncooked. However, when finely chopped and used judiciously, raw rosemary can be wonderful in a dressing; heating it very gently in oil is a good idea to get the flavour flowing.

- Tuck a few sprigs of rosemary inside and under a roasting chicken, or any joint of roasting meat. If you're stuffing a joint, add a stem or two to the middle before rolling up and tying.
- Stud a lamb joint with little sprigs of rosemary before roasting.
- Rosemary is also good with fish, particularly flaky white fish from the cod family. Trickle a gently infused rosemary and garlic oil over grilled or roast fillets, or add chopped rosemary to a breadcrumb crust for baked fish.
- Add large sprigs of rosemary to any tray of vegetables before roasting, particularly potatoes, pumpkin or parsnips.
- Infuse a lightly bruised stem or two of rosemary in a simmering soup, first tying it in a piece of muslin as the leaves have a tendency to break loose.

- Finely chopped rosemary is great in meaty stuffings. Here apple is a good complementary flavour, as are lemon and orange zests.
- **White beans with winter herbs** (p.204)
- **Soda bread with rosemary and sultanas** (p.212)
- **Rosemary focaccia** (p.209)
- **Rosemary and chilli oil** (p.238)
- **Pork with fennel and rosemary** (p.191)
- **Apple herb jelly** (p.232)

## How to grow

Rosemary is not the easiest herb to raise from seed and cultivars will not 'come true' from seed. If you're looking to buy a rosemary plant, you can't go wrong with the basic *Rosmarinus officinalis*, which is full of that classic pungent, piney rosemary flavour. However, there are some good cultivars. 'Tuscan Blue' tends to be less woody and has a slightly more lemony, peppery tone than the standard herb. 'Miss Jessop's Upright' is a striking plant that sends its stems straight up to the sky. It's more woody than some and needs lots of cutting, but this is handy if you actually want rosemary wood – to scent your barbecue, for instance, or to form skewers for threading kebabs. It also has a quite gingery scent. 'Prostratus Group', as the name suggests, has a low-growing, almost creeping habit and is great for pots or for trailing over a wall.

Rosemary is a Mediterranean herb and all varieties like full sun, a light, sandy soil and dry conditions. Growing the plant against a south-facing wall or fence, where it can soak up the sun and is protected from wind and rain, is a good idea. However, it is a hardy evergreen and will tolerate frost, snow and cold as long as it is not sitting in waterlogged ground. You should be able to harvest rosemary right through the winter. It also grows well in containers.

Rosemary is very prone to woodiness. If left to its own devices it eventually becomes a sort of tree. It can live for 20 or 30 years and there's nothing wrong with that if you've got the space for it but you'll get more abundant and tender leaves from a young managed plant. To keep it compact, avoid woodiness and promote lots of tender new growth, you need to keep cutting back. Proceed with caution, however. Drastic cutting back can kill or damage a plant, especially if done in autumn or winter. It's best to prune little and often (which is what you will be doing, in effect, if you use it regularly in the kitchen), rather than let it get too large then slash it back in one fell swoop.

If you have an overgrown rosemary bush, try cutting it gradually during spring and summer, without going right back into the old wood, allowing fresh new growth to come through in stages. In spring, you can use tender young cuttings to start new plants (see p.34), while the woodier trimmings make a fragrant fuel.

Sage *Salvia officinalis*

# Sage *Salvia officinalis*

| PLANT GROUP | Hardy evergreen perennial |
|---|---|
| HARVEST | All year round |

This pungent, spicy herb, with its slightly bitter camphorous quality, is a true stalwart. Not everyone loves it. Elizabeth David is among the many to have looked down her nose at it, and it is telling that it was used as a medicine rather than a foodstuff for centuries. But I think sage is definitely worth getting to grips with. It can be used all year round to give a deep savoury herbiness to rich and substantial dishes... it just needs to be added with a little care.

As with so many herbs, it's the mother species, the original model, that tends to give the best flavour. *Salvia officinalis*, with its velvety silver-green tongue-shaped leaves is a true friend in the kitchen, and my first choice for the garden. Variegated and fruit-scented sages, while pretty, are not so satisfactory for cooking, in my experience. You can find all sorts of 'exotics' – blackcurrant-, pineapple- or tangerine-scented sages, or species with purple, silver or red-splashed foliage. Among these, some have delicate heart-shaped leaves and, in many cases, the leaves have an astonishing scent – crush them between your fingers and you can drink in a burst of extraordinary fruity perfume. Their flowers are often gorgeous too – cerise or purple or scarlet. Any would make a wonderful addition to your garden but not necessarily to your kitchen patch.

## In the kitchen

Sage is strong stuff. Eat a leaf neat and you'll find it powerful and probably unpalatable. However, when used in small quantities, cooked and combined with other strong flavours, sage really shines. You can happily add it to a dish that will be cooked for some time, knowing that its flavour will inform the whole thing.

- A simple sage and onion stuffing is fantastic with pork, duck or goose. Finely chop 2 large onions and sauté in 25g butter and a dash of oil until really soft and golden. Allow to cool, then stir in 3 tbsp chopped sage, 75g fresh white breadcrumbs and enough beaten egg (1–2 large eggs) to make a sticky mixture that will hold together in a ball. Season well then form into balls and bake at 180°C/Gas mark 4 for 20–25 minutes.
- A simple sage butter – just a few slivered leaves warmed gently in barely foaming unsalted butter – is delicious spooned over homemade ravioli or any other fresh pasta, or freshly cooked gnocchi. Add a little grated Parmesan to finish.

- Sage has an amazing affinity with squashes. Toss cubed or sliced pumpkin or squash with a few smashed garlic cloves, lots of sage leaves, some olive or rapeseed oil and plenty of salt and pepper, then roast at 190°C/Gas mark 5 for 40–60 minutes until tender and caramelised. The squash (and the crisp, almost burnt sage leaves) can be eaten just as they are, thrown into a warm salad, a risotto or pasta dish, or puréed into a soup with some stock.
- A little chopped sage is lovely in homemade burgers.
- I love a saltimbocca with sage. Get a rose veal escalope and whack it gently with a mallet or pestle until nice and thin. Wrap a slice of air-dried ham around it and use a cocktail stick to secure a couple of sage leaves to it. Season, then fry in oil and butter. Remove from the pan and deglaze with marsala or white wine. Absolutely delicious with sagey roast potatoes.
- Sage leaves, briefly fried in hot oil until crisp, make a great garnish for a soup or risotto.
- You can add sage to a bouquet garni (see p.19) for flavouring soups, stews and slow-cooked beans.
- **Apple sauce with sage** (p.163)
- **White beans with winter herbs** (p.204)
- **Apple herb jelly** (p.232)

## How to grow

You can raise sage from spring-sown seed, take cuttings (see p.34) or buy young plants. Plant it out in a well-drained soil, in a sunny spot. It does well in a container, but you'll need a large one. As long as it's reasonably sheltered and the ground is not waterlogged, sage should be perfectly harvestable all year round. It's a great winter herb. My one caveat is that, in the winter, it can sometimes become overly camphorous in flavour. If this happens, wait for the new spring growth.

Sage will eventually become woody, and it's worth replacing plants every 4 or 5 years. To encourage bushy tender growth, cut it back hard in early spring, then keep cutting back the flowers through the growing season to maintain good leaf production (though it's worth letting it flower at least a little bit if you want to attract bees to your garden). Trim it back after flowering in late summer but before the cold weather.

Purple sage *Salvia officinalis* 'Purpurascens'

# Salad burnet *Sanguisorba minor*

| PLANT GROUP | Hardy evergreen perennial |
|-------------|---------------------------|
| HARVEST | All year round |

This very attractive plant looks diminutive and even fragile, but is actually quite a tough customer that will stay green and give you leaves all through the winter. For that reason alone, it is a very useful addition to any herb garden. The delicate cucumber-like flavour of its small, serrated leaves also offers a nice counterpoint to the strong, piney flavours of many other perennial herbs. It becomes slightly more bitter as the leaves age and the year progresses, but pleasantly so. Whatever the time of year, a confetti fall of little burnet leaves will enliven and undeniably prettify all kinds of dishes.

## In the kitchen

As the name suggests, this herb really is most at home tossed straight into a salad. I wouldn't cook it.

- Used raw and fresh, salad burnet will enhance any green salad, but is also good with sweet little cherry tomatoes, green beans or with cucumber.
- Add burnet to winter salads too; there are few flavours it will clash with. Try it with potatoes, aubergines, fennel or carrots.
- The leaves add a new dimension to sliced, lightly sugared strawberries.
- Salad burnet is also good added to cold drinks. Float some on a jug of Pimms, or use it in place of sorrel in the wine cup recipe on p.243.
- A few salad burnet leaves make a lovely garnish for a soup, whether it's a chilled summer broth or a hearty winter warmer.
- Combine salad burnet with parsley, chervil, chives and a little tarragon. Chop finely and stir into a warm white bean salad, with some rapeseed or extra virgin olive oil and a squeeze of lemon. This herb mix is also good stirred into cream cheese for sandwiches, or mayonnaise, or in an omelette.

## How to grow

Sow seeds in spring into plugs, or dig up an established plant in spring or autumn and divide it to create new ones. Salad burnet's natural habitat is chalky soil, but it should grow well in any free-draining ground. It's also good in containers. It likes sun or partial shade. Salad burnet looks delicate but is in fact very hardy – just keep cutting back the flowers to encourage leafy growth, or leave some at the end of the season if you want the plant to self-seed.

Scented geranium *Pelargonium graveolens*

# Scented geranium *Pelargonium*

| | |
|---|---|
| **PLANT GROUP** | Half-hardy evergreen perennial |
| **HARVEST** | All year round |

I've never particularly liked the scent of conventional garden geraniums, though I love their glorious flowers. With scented geraniums, the opposite is true. Their blooms are fairly forgettable but the scent of their leaves is unbeatable. It can be used to perfume cakes, syrups, sauces and jams – almost anything where the leaf can be infused, in fact.

It's the rose- and lemon-scented geraniums which are most useful to the cook. These have particularly intense fragrances which permeate and infuse well. Good examples include 'Attar of Roses' (*Pelargonium capitatum* 'Attar of Roses') and the rosy-citrusy *Pelargonium graveolens*, as well as the very lemony 'Mabel Grey' and 'Lara Nomad' varieties. I have also found the fruity scent of 'Big Apple' to carry successfully. But you can also buy pelargoniums that smell of peaches, various spices, peppermint, oranges and even chocolate – and many with intoxicating mingled scents that encompass several of the above.

If you get the chance to see the plant before you buy, crush a leaf gently between your fingers. If you are rewarded with a deep scent that pleases you, give it a try. Even if they don't prove pungent enough for culinary purposes, there's pleasure in simply liberating the scents from their handsome leaves with your fingertips. Some suppliers will also send you batches of fresh-cut leaves for cooking, so you don't necessarily have to invest in a plant to begin with (see Directory, p.248).

## In the kitchen

Scented geranium leaves should not actually be eaten: all of them are tough and not a little bitter, and some, such as the lemony *Pelargonium crispum* species, may cause stomach upsets if consumed in any quantity. Instead, the leaves are best infused into liquids.

Scented geraniums are particularly useful if you like the scent and flavour of roses in your cooking – roses themselves have only a short summer season, whereas a rose-tinged pelargonium will produce leaves all year.

- You may well have heard of the technique of using scented geranium leaves to line cake tins before baking, thereby giving a delicate perfume to the finished cake. I've done this but find the result is really too subtle. I prefer to use a scented geranium syrup (see overleaf) as a drizzle over the top of a freshly baked skewer-pierced cake.

Scented geranium 'Lara Nomad'

- For a scented geranium syrup, put 150g caster sugar and 150ml water into a saucepan. Heat gently, stirring often, until the sugar has dissolved, then increase the heat. Once simmering, cook the syrup for 5 minutes. Remove from the heat, add 2–3 large scented geranium leaves (or 5–6 small ones), giving them a bit of a twist and a crush in your hands first. Push the leaves down under the surface of the syrup. Leave to cool. This makes enough to drip and drizzle over one large plain cake. You can also use it on a fruit salad, or, diluted down a bit, for poaching fruit.
- A few lemon-scented leaves on the base of an apple, or apple and blackberry pie give a lovely new dimension to the fruit.
- **Sweet raspberry vinegar with scented geranium** (p.239)
- **Scented lemonade** (p.241)

## How to grow

These plants do not grow readily from seed, so buy young plants or take cuttings from established ones. Cuttings should be taken in late summer and sliced off cleanly with a knife, rather than leaving a heel, then follow the procedure on p.34.

Scented geraniums are best grown in pots, so you can easily control their environment. They must have free drainage so use a peat-free potting compost with a little fine sand mixed in. They are quite delicate but should be fine outside in a sheltered, sunny spot during good weather. However, they must be brought in before there's a chance of frost. They also do well in greenhouses, conservatories and other warm, light, protected places. I keep mine on a windowsill.

The greatest mistake is to confine them in too small a pot. Scented geraniums are expansive creatures and can grow pretty quickly, so give them room. They also really thrive on plenty of light. If, like me, you are absolutely terrible at remembering to water pot plants, make a diary or calendar note to do it regularly, i.e. before they're wilting! Give them an occasional feed too – well-diluted organic tomato feed or a spot of nettle tea, perhaps (see p.36), though this isn't ideal if you're growing indoors due to its penetrating aroma!

# Sorrel (broad-leaved) *Rumex acetosa*

| PLANT GROUP | Hardy perennial |
|---|---|
| HARVEST | April–October |

I never fail to be pleasantly shocked by just how sharp and lemony sorrel is. The name itself is derived from an old French word *surele*, meaning 'sour'. Small tender leaves are more gentle, while large mature leaves can almost overpower the taste buds. Although you can sometimes buy the fresh leaves, sorrel is a very easy and forgiving plant to grow, pushing up its leaves well into the colder weather, then obligingly reappearing in spring, whether you tend it carefully or not.

Sorrel is also a leaf that grows abundantly in the wild in Britain, in grassy places, hedgerows and on heathland. It makes a lovely wild harvest and is worth looking out for from March onwards, always bearing in mind good foraging etiquette – tread carefully, pick sparingly. Make sure you don't confuse it with Lords and Ladies, which has similar-looking leaves, and is poisonous. Take a good illustrated forager's guide with you, such as John Wright's *River Cottage Hedgerow Handbook* (see Directory, p.249).

## In the kitchen

This tender arrow-shaped leaf is half herb, half salad, and deliciously refreshing however you use it. Combined with a few other herbs, baby sorrel leaves make a wonderful mini-salad – the sort of tiny tangle of green leaves that goes well alongside something rich. Or you can shred it into more substantial leafy salads with lettuces, spring onions, eggs and/or potatoes.

The flavour of grown-up sorrel is also robust enough for a bit of light cooking. Stir the shredded leaves into a risotto, soup or omelette for the last few minutes to transform the flavour. In all cases, exercise a little caution: taste the raw leaf first to ascertain how astringent it is. Different plants at different times of year can vary quite a bit, depending on the levels of oxalic acid they contain. This acid, also found in spinach, is responsible for the leaf's sharp sourness. In large quantities, it is actually poisonous – but you'd have to eat a lot to be affected (best not give it to your tortoise, though). Use sorrel as soon as you can after picking – it wilts quickly. When cooked, it collapses to a fraction of its former volume, and will also turn from bright green to dull khaki.

- For a tasty lentil and sorrel soup, simmer brown lentils in water until very soft, then purée. Reheat, adding plenty of chopped sorrel, some double cream and seasoning.

- Stir a couple of generous handfuls of shredded sorrel into freshly cooked hot new potatoes, along with some seasoning and a splosh of olive oil.
- **Simple herb salad** (p.175)
- **Sorrel sauce** (p.164)
- **Sorrel wine cup** (p.243)

## How to grow

Sorrel is easily raised from seeds – just sow in plugs in the spring. It tends to grow abundantly in most situations but it prefers a rich, damp soil and partial shade. Cut back its tall flowering spikes to promote leafy growth and don't be worried about razing the whole lot to the ground during the season to stimulate the production of a new crop of baby leaves. Once established, sorrel will come back year after year, but it's worth replacing often as young plants have the best flavour.

## Relatives

French or buckler-leaf sorrel (*Rumex scutatus*) has a shorter, rounder leaf. Its flavour is a little less astringent and powerful than the broad-leaved variety. Wood sorrel (*Oxalis acetosella*) is a tiny, delicate, trefoil-leaved plant found in woodland all over Britain. It has a similar lemon-sharp flavour to broad-leaved sorrel.

Sorrel *Rumex acetosa*

Shredding sorrel

# Summer savory *Satureja hortensis*

| PLANT GROUP | Hardy annual |
|---|---|
| HARVEST | May–September |

This is a very attractive herb, with slender upright stalks that bear pretty little flowers. The flavour is definitely in the 'woody' category: strongly aromatic, slightly peppery and piney, with hints of black tea. It is a native of hot places, including Greece, where it is said the satyrs grazed on it, hence the Latin name.

## In the kitchen

Summer savory is rather like thyme in the flavours it complements – everything from green veg to chicken and fish, cheese and cream. However, savory can have a slightly piney edge that thyme does not, so I wouldn't use it in very delicate dishes such as salads or omelettes. Summer savory can be added during or after cooking. If you do both, you'll get layers of flavour. If you are adding late-season leaves to a dish at the end of cooking, chop them very finely as they can be a little tough.

- Add finely chopped summer savory to homemade sausages, burgers, pâtés, potted meats or meat stuffings. I particularly like it combined with some sautéed finely chopped onion and garlic and used to flavour lamb burgers.
- Try summer savory stirred into a tomato sauce or soup – add some at the beginning of cooking and a pinch more at the end.
- After frying pork chops, chicken breasts or veal escalopes, deglaze the pan with a little white wine, then add 1 tbsp chopped summer savory and a splosh of cream. Simmer briefly and season before pouring over the meat.
- The pungency of summer savory makes it a good foil to creamy and earthy flavours – try adding a chopped tablespoonful to the garlic-infused cream for a classic potato gratin.
- **Runner beans with summer savory** (p.203)

## How to grow

I've not had any trouble raising summer savory from seed, sown in the spring into plugs. It prefers a sunny spot on light, well-drained soil. It's also great in a pot and can be grown on a windowsill. Extend its short life by pinching out flowering tips as soon as they appear.

## Relatives

Winter savory, see p.155.

# Sweet cicely *Myrrhis odorata*

| PLANT GROUP | Hardy perennial |
|---|---|
| HARVEST | Leaves: March–October |
| | Seeds: June–September |

In late spring, when its frothy white flowers are at their peak and the frondy leaves at their lush green best, sweet cicely is one of the prettiest things you can have in your herb garden. The leaves have a delicate honeyed anise quality. The large seeds, harvested green and juicy rather than dried, can be used in cooking too.

## In the kitchen

Sweet cicely has much in common with chervil. The flavour is sweeter but it has the same subtle, aniseedy note and is similarly used in salads, mayonnaise and omelettes. It is also one of those herbs that reduces acidity in other ingredients, so is often cooked with gooseberries, rhubarb, cooking apples or blackcurrants, and means the dish needs less sugar. The green seeds work very well used in this way.

- I really like sweet cicely in a flavoured butter with some seasoning and lemon juice, tossed into freshly cooked vegetables, or smeared on chicken.
- For a gooseberry and sweet cicely compote, top and tail 500g gooseberries and put in a pan with 2 tbsp sugar, 2 tbsp water and 2 tbsp finely chopped sweet cicely (leaves and/or seed pods). Bring to a simmer and cook for a few minutes, until soft. Taste and add more sugar if you like (a lot depends on the variety of gooseberry). Well chilled, this is lovely with a spoonful of yoghurt or cream, or you can use it to make a crumble (serving 2–3).
- This herb's sweetness means it contributes something very pleasant to drinks. Try it in a wine cup (see p.243).
- **Rhubarb crumble with angelica** (p.223)

## How to grow

Sweet cicely seeds must be sown outside in the autumn as they need several months of low temperatures before they will germinate. Choose a partially shaded site, with rich, moist but well-drained soil. This isn't a herb for container-growing as its long root needs plenty of depth. However, in a suitable bed it is a plant that will provide leaves for the greater part of the year. As with so many herbs, cutting it back after flowering will promote the growth of fresh new leaves. The flowers themselves are very pretty and, if left, will form elegant elongated seeds. These can be harvested and used fresh for flavouring. Any seed left on the plant will sow itself quite readily.

Sweet cicely seeds

# Tarragon (French)
*Artemesia dracunculus*

| PLANT GROUP | Half-hardy perennial |
|---|---|
| HARVEST | May–September |

Cold chicken, cold new potatoes, mayonnaise, lots of chopped fresh tarragon…
if there is a better summer lunch, I do not know of it. This feathery-leaved plant is
queen of all the anise-scented herbs and an ingredient in many classic dishes with
very good reason – the unique flavour is quite penetrating and tenacious but still
manages to be delicate and refined. That anise quality acts as both flavour and
seasoning. It rarely overpowers but enhances, defines and enlivens a dish.

## In the kitchen
A little tarragon can sometimes go a long way but, at the same time, it's not a herb
you necessarily need to hold back with. Adding an excessive quantity to something
won't make it taste unpleasant, just very tarragony. This is a herb that can withstand
a bit of cooking but in reality you are more likely to use tarragon in a raw or lightly
cooked form.

- To make a lovely tarragon vinegar, fantastic in dressings, mayonnaises
  or sauces, just loosely pack a clean jam jar with tarragon leaves. Cover
  completely with white wine vinegar and leave at room temperature for
  2 weeks before straining into a sterilised bottle and sealing.
- Tarragon is lovely with all sorts of green vegetables. I particularly like
  it with beans. Try adding sliced runner or green beans to a pan of soft
  sweated onions, along with a little water. Cook until the beans are just
  tender, then finish with salt and pepper, a squeeze of lemon and plenty
  of chopped tarragon.
- Combine tarragon with parsley, chives and chervil to create the classic
  blend *fines herbes* – exceptionally good in an omelette (see p.182).
- For a tasty supper, brown some chicken joints, then place in a roasting tin.
  Deglaze the browning pan with white wine and add to the tin. Season the
  chicken well and roast until golden and cooked through. Strew lots of
  roughly chopped tarragon over the chicken, leave for a few minutes so the
  flavours begin to release, then serve with bread or crushed new potatoes.
- **Tarragon mayonnaise** (p.159)
- **Béarnaise sauce** (p.160)

- Creamed swiss chard (p.208)
- Tarragon eggs (p.184)
- Herb omelette (p.182)

## How to grow

French tarragon likes full sun and well-drained soil and does not thrive at all in cold, wet conditions. I have grown it successfully in pots, but it needs space and can easily become pot-bound.

Tarragon rarely produces seed, but propagates itself via underground runners. It's easy to start new plants from these runners yourself. Just dig up an established tarragon plant in the spring and you will see white growing shoots among the roots. Ease the roots apart and break off small sections with shoots attached. Replant the root/shoot sections, completely covering them with compost, and keep just moist. New green shoots should soon appear. This process is worth doing every few years because older tarragon plants lose their flavour.

## Relatives

The similar-looking Russian tarragon (*Artemesia dracunculoides*) has an inferior flavour, as its nickname 'false tarragon' suggests.

**Tarragon** *Artemesia dracunculus*

Thyme *Thymus vulgaris*

# Thyme and lemon thyme
*Thymus vulgaris; Thymus* x *citriodorus*

| PLANT GROUP | Hardy evergreen perennial |
|---|---|
| HARVEST | All year round |

Thyme is a precious ingredient, one whose fragrant woody, smoky taste pretty much epitomises the 'herby' flavour that we crave in some dishes. It has the same fundamental usefulness as bay in the way it infuses a lovely note into stocks, soups, stews, dressings, stuffings and a multitude of other dishes. But it's more versatile: you can eat it raw or cooked, add it finely chopped for a really thymey hit, or keep a sprig whole for a more subtle effect.

## In the kitchen
You really can't go wrong with thyme: raw or cooked, generous or judicious, it's rarely going to do anything but enhance a dish. It's a fiddly one, though – removing the tiny leaves from the stems can be tricky. If you have very tender sprigs of thyme, you can finely chop the whole lot, stem and all, into a dish. If you have a woody sprig, pick off the leaves as best you can with your fingertips but accept that you may not get every one. Tougher stalks are really not nice to eat, but, even with most of the leaves removed, they are perfectly good for infusing in things.

- I always like to add a sprig of thyme to a simmering stock or a bouquet garni (see p.19).
- Put a few sprigs of thyme into the cavity of a chicken before roasting and flavour butter to stuff under the skin with chopped thyme (see p.198).
- Finely chopped thyme is fantastic added to savoury dumplings to go on top of a stew.
- Tiny whole fresh thyme leaves are delicious scattered over a tomato salad.
- Thyme is a must with roasted or braised root vegetables, especially pungent roots, such as swede, parsnip and celeriac, as well as beetroot and kohlrabi.
- Roughly crushed thyme leaves add a great deal of character to marinades and dressings.
- Thyme flowers are beautiful and the perfect edible garnish for a homemade pizza or bruschetta.
- **Soda bread with thyme, Cheddar and mustard** (p.212)
- **Apple herb jelly** (p.232)
- **Salmoriglio sauce** (p.165)
- **Loin of lamb with lavender and lemon thyme** (p.194)

## How to grow

I have struggled a little with growing thyme. The plants always start off well but seem to become twiggy, unproductive and rather morose within a year or so. I think this is because, despite being a hardy perennial, it really hankers for the hot, dry thin-soiled hillsides of its native lands. It intensely resents our wet winters and it doesn't really like being cut too much. My approach now is to focus on young tender-stemmed plants, and not to expect too much of them in terms of longevity.

You can grow *Thymus vulgaris* from seed and this is one way to maintain a good supply, although the plants are slow to develop. Sow them indoors in plugs in the spring, in a warm place, and don't transplant them outside until the weather is warm and the plants seem robust – even if that isn't until the following spring. Make sure you harden them off (see p.33).

Thyme loves warmth and well-drained poor soil and hates prolonged contact with frost, rain and wind. Plant it in a sheltered but sunny position. Apart from when first planting, keep watering to a minimum. In the summer, cut it regularly but not too drastically and trim back after flowering to encourage new growth. However, keep cutting to a minimum in winter when you may find it stops growing almost completely.

Thyme grows well in containers, so having some in a pot on a windowsill is one way to help ensure fresh thyme through the winter.

## Relatives

There are a huge number of thyme varieties, many of them very beautiful and fragrant. However, few species hit the culinary spot in the same way as the good old *Thymus vulgaris*. One notable exception is lemon thyme (*Thymus* x *citriodorus*). It is so intensely flavoured – pungently lemony, with that warm, woody thyme backnote – that it really functions as a completely different herb in its own right.

Lemon thyme is delicious but should be used fairly carefully because it is so strong. I love it in stuffings, or combined with soft sweated onions then mixed with wilted chopped spinach, but you can also use it to perfume a custard or cake batter. If you can't get hold of lemon thyme when a recipe calls for it, you can use ordinary thyme combined with finely grated lemon zest. The flavour will not be the same, but you'll be in the right ballpark.

I also like orange thyme (*Thymus fragrantissimus*). Crushing it in your hands releases the most wonderful dry, warm, spicy fragrance, which you can capture by infusing it in olive oil with some garlic (as for the rosemary and chilli oil on p.238), or by beating it into soft butter with orange zest, chilli and black pepper.

Lemon thyme *Thymus* x *citriodorus*

# Welsh onion *Allium fistulosum*

| PLANT GROUP | Hardy perennial |
|---|---|
| HARVEST | All year round |

This handsome allium offers a lot: you can eat the young and the mature stems, as well as the flowers. It has real presence in the garden too, looking rather like a giant thick-shafted chive, and producing a similar flower from its second year onwards. It doesn't form an actual bulb but you can pull the whole stem out to use like a thick spring onion or, alternatively, cut the young stem tops like chives. You can eat the flowers too, separated into their little individual parts.

The name is slightly misleading as this allium has nothing in particular to do with Wales. 'Welsh' is believed to be a corruption of the German *walsch*, meaning foreign. In fact, the plant hails from Siberia. It is also known as the Japanese leek and the bunching onion.

## In the kitchen

You can eat the stems of the Welsh onion raw, slicing them thinly and scattering into salads or over pizza. They have quite a strong oniony punch, which you may find delicious. I've never been much of a fan of raw onion, so I prefer them cooked. Sliced thinly and sautéed gently in butter with a pinch of salt and a dash of oil, you can use them in a hundred different ways.

Once the onion is flowering, the stalk will harden and become unpalatable, but the flower itself, pinched apart into little white flowerlets, makes a delicious and pretty oniony sprinkle that can be used much like chive flowers (see p.63). I particularly like them on vegetable risottos.

- Use sautéed Welsh onion as the first layer of a pizza topping. Try layering thinly sliced cooked new potatoes, thyme and a rich melting cheese, such as mozzarella or Stinking Bishop, on top.
- Blind bake a 25cm pastry crust and fill with as many sautéed Welsh onions as you can, or combine with other alliums such as shallots, spring onions or green garlic. Then add some grated flavoursome cheese and pour on a well-seasoned custard (200ml whole milk beaten with 200ml double cream, 2 whole eggs and 1 extra egg yolk). Bake at 180°C/Gas mark 4 for around 35 minutes until golden and just set.
- For a simple light onion soup, sauté Welsh onions until very soft, then add a splash of white wine and some well-flavoured chicken stock and simmer for another 30 minutes or so. Season and serve with croûtons.

- For a very simple and lovely supper, stir cooked Welsh onions into hot pasta with a splosh of cream and some chopped black olives.

## How to grow

Sow Welsh onion seeds outside in March or April, directly into their growing site, which should have well-drained, rich soil and sun or partial shade. The Welsh onion is a hardy herb that you should be able to harvest even in the depths of winter, but bear in mind it needs to be well watered and weeded during the summer. It should then produce more and more stems year by year. Take care when pulling up the stems for eating, as you don't want to damage those left in the ground. Cut back spent stalks completely after flowering to allow new shoots to come through, and divide large clumps after a few years to promote vigorous fresh growth.

## Relatives

The tree onion (*Allium cepa* Proliferum group) is a not dissimilar plant which has the distinction of producing bulbs at the top end of its stalk which grow crazily, sending their tendrils out into the air. Each of these baby bulbs, which you should get in the second year of growth, can be plucked and eaten, or planted to produce a new plant. You can eat the stems too.

Welsh onion *Allium fistulosum*

Welsh onion flowers

# Wild garlic *Allium ursinum*

| PLANT GROUP | Hardy perennial |
| --- | --- |
| HARVEST | March–May |

From March to May this delicious wild food – also known as ramsons, bear garlic or wood garlic – appears in dense patches in damp, shady, wooded places. The powerful garlicky scent is unmistakable. Its elegant stems, delicate tulip-like leaves, bulbs and, later in the season, starry white flowers, are all edible, but if you're gathering this herb wild, it's best to leave the bulbs untouched for next year's crop. Wild garlic grows throughout Europe but is localised. However, once you've found a patch, you should be able to return year after year for a harvest.

## In the kitchen
Quite pungent but subtly different to conventional garlic, wild garlic is more like a strong, garlicky chive. It quickly loses its flavour on cooking, so is best eaten raw or only lightly cooked. Roll up the leaves and slice them across into thin ribbons. Add to dishes at the end of cooking, or scatter on just before serving.

* For an easy soup, simmer potato and onion or leek in chicken or veg stock, adding shredded wild garlic at the end. Purée, finish with cream and season.
* Try stirring shredded wild garlic into a risotto at the last minute. This is particularly good with a chicken or mushroom risotto.
* Wild garlic flowers look really pretty on a salad or homemade pizza.
* Use wild garlic to replace chives or garlic chives in any recipe.
* **Spring pasta with wild garlic and purple sprouting broccoli** (p.199)
* **Herb omelette** (p.182)
* **Walnut and wild garlic pesto** (p.166)
* **Herb noodle soup** (p.173)

## How to grow
Wild garlic is easy to cultivate but it's invasive so be cautious. Buy seeds or gather them from wild flowerheads, sow directly in a shady and slightly damp spot in the autumn and they should shoot up the following spring. You can also buy young plants. Once established, future work is more likely to be taming than encouraging.

## Relatives
Three-cornered garlic (*Allium triquetrum*), with its distinctive triangular cross-section stem, is similarly delicious and can be used in much the same way.

# Winter savory *Satureja montana*

| PLANT GROUP | Hardy evergreen perennial |
|---|---|
| HARVEST | All year round |

Evergreen winter savory is a very attractive plant with dark, glossy needle-like leaves. Stronger and more pungent than its summer cousin, it is piney, a little like a combination of mint, pepper and thyme, with hints of menthol and a cleansing, almost tingling effect in the mouth if you sample it raw.

## In the kitchen
The name says it all really: winter savory is definitely one for cold-weather cooking and comfort food. It's an excellent partner to red meats, dried pulses and winter vegetables. Chop the leaves fairly finely and add in small quantities, or use it as an infusing herb in a bouquet garni (see p.19).

- Add chopped winter savory to homemade sausages, burgers and pâtés.
- Finely chopped, this is a very good herb for meat stuffings.
- **Stuffed breast of lamb with dried apricots and winter savory** (p.193)
- **White beans with winter herbs** (p.204)

## How to grow
If you want to grow this herb from seed, sow indoors in early spring and just press the seeds lightly into the compost but leave them uncovered, as they need light to germinate. The young plants will need hardening off before planting out (see p.33). You can also take spring cuttings of winter savory (see p.34).

Like its summer sibling, winter savory prefers a warm, sunny position on light, well-drained soil. I have grown it very successfully in a pot on the patio where it seems happy to keep going all year round as long as it doesn't get too dry and I keep cutting from it, little and often, but more cautiously in the winter.

## Relatives
Summer savory, see p.141.

Recipes

# Mayonnaise

A good homemade mayonnaise recipe is a great thing to have in your repertoire. It's particularly useful for the summer months when you can lace it with herbs of your choice and serve it with all kinds of vegetables, salads, fish, eggs and meat.

*Makes about 300ml, enough for 6–8*

½ small garlic clove
2 large egg yolks
½ tsp English mustard
1 tsp white wine vinegar (or
    tarragon vinegar, see p.144)

About 250ml light olive oil,
    or 100ml extra virgin olive oil
    blended with 150ml sunflower oil
Sea salt and freshly ground
    black pepper

Crush the garlic with a good pinch of salt (see p.20). Scrape into a bowl and add the egg yolks, mustard, vinegar and some pepper.

Start whisking in the oil, a few drops at a time to start with, then in small dashes, whisking in each addition so it is fully amalgamated. Stop when you have a glossy, wobbly mayonnaise. Taste and add more salt, pepper and vinegar as required.

## Variations

Flavour the basic mayonnaise generously with any of the following chopped herbs, adding at least a good 2 tbsp:

**Chives** Essential for a new potato salad.

**Tarragon** Lovely with eggs, chicken or potatoes.

**Basil** Fantastic with tomatoes or in sandwiches with cold chicken or ham.

**Parsley** A versatile mayonnaise to go with most things. For a garlic and parsley mayo, increase the garlic to a whole clove; this is good with shellfish or you can use it as the base for a tartare sauce.

**Chervil and lemon zest** Particularly good with green beans, asparagus, potatoes, cold chicken, fish or shellfish.

# Béarnaise sauce

This classic velvety sauce is delicate but rich and fragrant with tarragon. Serve it with simply cooked steak, trout or chicken.

*Serves 4*

1 medium shallot, peeled and finely chopped
A few black peppercorns
2 tbsp white wine vinegar
2 tbsp dry white wine
2 tbsp chopped tarragon
2 tsp chopped chervil (optional)

2 large egg yolks, at room temperature
150g unsalted butter, melted and slightly cooled
A pinch of sugar
Sea salt and freshly ground black pepper

Put the shallot, peppercorns, wine vinegar, wine, 1 tbsp of the chopped tarragon, and the chervil, if using, into a small saucepan. Bring to a simmer and cook for a few minutes until the liquid has reduced to 1 tbsp. Tip into a sieve over a bowl, pressing the shallot mixture to extract every last drop of juice. Leave to cool.

Add the egg yolks to the cooled liquor and whisk together. Now slowly whisk in the warm melted butter, little by little, to form a smooth emulsion, rather like a very loose mayonnaise. Stir in the remaining chopped tarragon and season to taste with salt and pepper, and a pinch of sugar if necessary.

Serve the sauce pretty much straight away (though you can keep it warm in a bowl over a saucepan of hot water for a little while).

# Salmoriglio sauce

I love the slightly bitter, smoky tang of oregano in this Sicilian-style sauce. You only need a little bit to deliciously dress a piece of barbecued fish or roast lamb.

*Serves 4*

2 tbsp finely chopped oregano
1 tbsp finely chopped thyme
Grated zest of ½ lemon, plus
    a squeeze of juice
1 small garlic clove, very finely
    chopped

1 tsp Dijon mustard
4 tbsp olive oil
A pinch of sugar
Sea salt and freshly ground
    black pepper

Put the oregano, thyme, lemon zest and garlic into a small bowl and mix well. Add a squeeze of lemon juice, the mustard, olive oil, sugar and some salt and pepper and mix well. Taste and add more salt, pepper and/or lemon juice as needed.

# Skordalia

This Greek dip is ridiculously garlicky. Actually, this version uses less garlic than many, but it's still pretty powerful stuff and possibly not ideal before a big date! But I love its rich, oily, sweet, strong taste, especially with contrasting foods such as raw fennel or carrots. Other crudités work well too and it's traditionally served with roasted beetroot.

*Serves 4–6 as an accompaniment*

50g whole blanched almonds,
    lightly toasted and cooled
50g fresh white breadcrumbs
2 fat garlic cloves, peeled and
    crushed

2 tsp red wine vinegar
About 100ml extra virgin olive oil
Sea salt and freshly ground
    black pepper

Put the toasted almonds, breadcrumbs, garlic, wine vinegar and some salt and pepper into a food processor and whiz until the nuts are finely chopped. Transfer to a dish and gradually stir in the extra virgin olive oil until you have a thick, oily purée. Taste and adjust the seasoning, adding a little more vinegar if you like.

# Basil and parsley pesto

The classic Italian *pesto alla Genovese* is made with basil and pine nuts, and extremely fine it is too. But the idea can be adapted to other herbs, and other nuts, as you'll see here. I particularly like the combination of basil and parsley, though you can use parsley alone. You can also use mint in a pesto, or stronger herbs, such as sage or thyme, though these are best combined with parsley so they don't overpower the sauce. As well as being excellent with pasta, pestos make a superb finishing touch to soups. They are also good with steak or chicken, delicious smeared over roasted vegetables and lovely as a simple dip with crudités.

*Makes enough for pasta for 4*

50g pine nuts, lightly toasted
30g bunch of basil, leaves only
30g bunch of flat-leaf parsley,
    leaves only
1 garlic clove, peeled and
    chopped

35g Parmesan, finely grated
Finely grated zest of ½ lemon
100–150ml extra virgin olive oil
A good squeeze of lemon juice
Sea salt and freshly ground
    black pepper

First toast the pine nuts: put them in a dry frying pan and toast over a medium heat for a few minutes, tossing frequently, until golden brown. Remove them from the pan immediately, so they don't burn, and leave to cool.

Put the toasted nuts into a food processor, along with the basil, parsley, garlic, Parmesan and lemon zest. Blitz to a paste. Then, with the motor running, slowly pour in the extra virgin olive oil until you have a thick, sloppy purée.

Scrape the pesto into a bowl. Season with salt and pepper and add a good squeeze of lemon juice to taste. This pesto will keep in a jar in the fridge for a few days.

## Variation

Walnut and wild garlic pesto  Replace the pine nuts with walnuts, lightly toasted in an oven preheated to 180°C/Gas mark 4 for 5–8 minutes. Replace the basil and parsley with roughly chopped wild garlic leaves and stems.

# Carrot soup with dill
## and mustard

Carrot and coriander soup is a ubiquitous dish with good reason, as it's very tasty. You certainly could use coriander here. However, the clean freshness of dill is lovely with the sweetness of carrots.

*Serves 4–6*

2 tbsp rapeseed or olive oil
1 onion, peeled and sliced
1 celery stick, sliced
500g carrots, peeled and sliced
800ml chicken or vegetable stock,
    or water, or a mixture

15–20g bunch of dill
1 heaped tsp Dijon mustard
2 heaped tbsp crème fraîche
Sea salt and freshly ground
    black pepper

Heat the oil in a large saucepan over a medium heat. Add the onion, celery and carrots. Once they start to sizzle, reduce the heat, cover the pan and sweat the veg, stirring once or twice, for 10 minutes. Add the stock and/or water. Bring to a simmer and cook for 12–15 minutes, or until the carrots are tender.

Meanwhile, cut the top quarter off the bunch of dill and set aside for serving. Discard the stalks from the remaining dill, then roughly chop the frondy leaves.

Add the chopped dill to the soup and simmer for another 2 minutes only. Add the mustard, then purée the soup in a blender. Return to the pan and season well with salt and pepper. Reheat if necessary.

Serve the soup in warmed bowls, topped with the crème fraîche. Finish with the remaining dill and a good grinding of pepper.

# Chervil soup

Rich, deeply coloured and intense, this is ideal to serve in small portions as a starter. And since chervil can be persuaded to grow all year round (see p.60), you can enjoy this as a summer or winter dish.

*Serves 4 as a starter*

50g unsalted butter
5 shallots, peeled and thinly sliced
1 inner celery stick, thinly sliced
500ml chicken or vegetable stock
150g bunch of chervil
2 egg yolks

50ml double cream, plus a little
    extra to finish
A squeeze of lemon juice
Sea salt and freshly ground
    black pepper

Melt the butter in a saucepan over a low heat. Add the shallots and celery and sweat, covered, for about 10 minutes. Add the stock, bring to the boil, then reduce the heat and simmer for about 10 minutes.

Separate out a small handful of the chervil and set aside. Roughly chop the rest, stalks and all, and add to the saucepan. Once the stock has returned to a simmer, cook for just 1–2 minutes, then remove from the heat. Transfer to a blender and purée until smooth. Return to a clean pan.

Whisk the egg yolks and cream together, then whisk into the soup. Reheat gently, stirring constantly, until just below a simmer; don't let it get to simmering point. The egg yolk will thicken the soup slightly. Season with salt, pepper and a squeeze of lemon juice to taste.

Pick the leaves from the reserved chervil and chop finely, or leave whole if you prefer. Serve the soup in warmed bowls, finished with the extra chervil and a little swirl of cream.

# Celery leaf and lovage soup

This is a creamy, deeply flavoured soup – perfect for lunch on a cold day. Try it with a hunk of homemade soda bread, either plain or herby (see p.212). Alternatively, make the soup even more hearty with a scattering of croûtons or chopped ham.

*Serves 4*

A knob of unsalted butter
2 tbsp rapeseed or olive oil
2 leeks, trimmed, well washed
   and sliced
1 garlic clove, peeled and sliced
3–4 slender stems of celery leaf,
   leaves separated, stems
   chopped

400g potato (1 large one), peeled
   and cut into large pieces
1 litre chicken stock
1 tbsp roughly chopped lovage
1 good tsp Dijon mustard
4–5 tbsp double cream
Sea salt and freshly ground
   black pepper

Melt the butter with the oil in a pan over a medium heat. Add the leeks, garlic and the chopped celery leaf stems. Cover the pan, reduce the heat and sweat together for about 10 minutes, until soft. Add the potato and the stock. Bring to a simmer and cook, covered, for about 12 minutes, until the potato is soft. Scoop out the pieces of potato with a slotted spoon and set aside.

Roughly chop the celery leaves and combine with the chopped lovage. You should have 2–3 tbsp chopped herbs altogether. Add to the soup, along with a good pinch of salt and lots of freshly ground pepper. Purée, using a blender. Return the soup to the pan.

Put the potato through a ricer (or push through a sieve), back into the soup. Stir until incorporated. Reheat if necessary, then stir in the mustard and cream. Taste and adjust the seasoning, then serve.

# Herb noodle soup

This is so simple and quick, and yet so satisfying. It's soothing comfort food, but actually quite light and delicate at the same time. You can use various different herbs, depending on what you have to hand. I've given the recipe in a one-person quantity as it's the sort of dish you might make for yourself when eating alone after a hard day. But just increase the quantities to scale it up for more people. If you want to make the dish vegetarian, replace the chicken stock with vegetable stock, and the chicken with tofu.

*Herbs to use (alone or in combination)*
**Shredded wild garlic**
**Shredded basil or Thai basil**
**Finely chopped lemongrass leaves or stem**
**Shredded mint**
**Snipped chives or garlic chives**
**Chopped coriander**
**Shredded perilla**

*Serves 1*

**400ml good chicken stock**
**A little deseeded and finely sliced red chilli**
**1 small garlic clove, sliced**
**50g dried egg noodles**
**About 50g cold cooked chicken, shredded or cubed**

**About 3 tbsp chopped or shredded herbs (see above)**
**Optional seasonings: soy sauce, lemon or lime juice, toasted sesame oil**
**Sea salt and freshly ground black pepper**

Put the stock, chilli and garlic into a saucepan and bring to a simmer. Season with salt and pepper to taste. Use your hands to break up the noodles as much as you can, dropping them into the simmering stock as you go. Once back up to a simmer, cook for about 3 minutes, stirring to break up the noodles.

Add the chicken and simmer for another minute, to heat it through, then add the herbs and immediately turn off the heat. Taste again and adjust the seasoning – you could add a dash of soy sauce if you like or perhaps a squeeze of lemon or lime juice, or a dash of toasted sesame oil.

Serve the soup straight away, piping hot, in a deep bowl. Slurping is unavoidable.

# Simple herb salad

Although this looks rather summery, I actually came up with it in October, when all the ingredients were still going strong in my garden. It's a fresh and delicate little dish, ideal as a very simple starter or a palate-cleanser between richer courses.

*Per person*

A small handful of tender sorrel
   leaves, stalks removed
A few sprigs of chervil (leaves only)
3–4 chives, snipped into 2–3cm
   lengths

A little extra virgin olive or
   rapeseed oil
About 6 borage flowers

Arrange the sorrel leaves on each serving plate, or on a larger platter, then add the chervil and snipped chives. Sprinkle a little oil over the salad, then finish with the borage flowers.

# Apple and celery leaf salad
## with Cheddar and walnuts

This super-simple little salad relies on the wonderful affinity between apples and celery. A bit of nutty Cheddar finishes the whole thing nicely. I could easily polish off this quantity myself, but it would make a nice starter for two.

*Serves 1–2*

1 crisp, tart dessert apple,
   such as Cox
A squeeze of lemon or orange juice
1 tbsp finely chopped celery leaf
   and stem

About 50g strongish Cheddar, diced
A few walnuts, roughly chopped
Sea salt and freshly ground
   black pepper

Core and chop the apple (there's no need to peel it) and toss immediately with the lemon or orange juice to prevent browning. Stir in the chopped celery leaf and stem, the Cheddar, walnuts and a little salt and pepper to taste. Serve straight away with a chunk of well-buttered wholemeal bread on the side.

# Green and gold salad

Try serving this as part of a spread of dips, breads and mezze or tapas. The orange flower water has a unique way of lifting and subtly perfuming the salad, but you could use a squeeze of orange juice instead.

*Serves 4*

2 tbsp olive oil
½ tsp orange flower water
A squeeze of lemon juice
4 handfuls lamb's lettuce, or another
   mild, tender leaf, such as purslane

About 50 small, young marigold
   leaves
4 marigold flowers
Sea salt and freshly ground
   black pepper

Mix the olive oil, orange flower water, lemon juice and some seasoning together to make a dressing. Put the lamb's lettuce or other salad leaves and marigold leaves into a bowl and toss lightly with the dressing (you might not need it all). Arrange on a serving plate. Pull the petals from the flowers, scatter over the leaves and serve.

# Crab and broad bean salad

This is lovely served as an elegant starter. It's delicious when made in the summer with freshly picked baby broad beans, but it's also successful with frozen ones.

*Serves 2*

200g podded broad beans (small
   ones if possible)
About 100g fresh brown and white
   crabmeat (1 small crab should
   be about right)

A handful of tender chervil sprigs
A little extra virgin olive oil
A squeeze of lemon juice
Sea salt and freshly ground
   black pepper

Bring a pan of water to the boil. Add the broad beans and cook until tender – just a couple of minutes for fresh little ones. Drain and, when cool enough to handle, pop the beans out of their skins.

Arrange the broad beans and crabmeat in separate piles on individual plates. Add a little pile of chervil sprigs. Trickle the whole thing with some extra virgin olive oil, a good spritz of lemon and some salt and pepper, then serve.

# Herby chicken noodle salad

The pungent aromatic herbs used in this flavour-packed, generous salad are no mere garnish; they form a crucial part of the body of the dish so don't hold back. You could use even more than I suggest here.

*Serves 4*

200g rice noodles
150g mangetout, sugarsnap peas
   or green beans
200g cold cooked chicken, roughly
   shredded or chopped
3 tbsp shredded basil or, even better,
   Thai basil
3 tbsp roughly chopped coriander
3 tbsp shredded spearmint
75g cashew nuts, lightly toasted

*For the dressing*

1 tbsp soy sauce
2 tsp clear honey
1 garlic clove, peeled and grated
1 good tsp grated root ginger
1 red chilli, deseeded and very
   finely chopped
Juice of 1 lime
4 tbsp sunflower oil

For the dressing, put all the ingredients into a screw-topped jar, secure the lid and shake well to combine and emulsify.

Cook the rice noodles according to the pack instructions. Drain, rinse under cold water and drain well again, then transfer to a bowl and add the dressing. Toss well.

Steam or simmer the mangetout, sugarsnaps or beans very briefly, until just tender but still crunchy. Drain, refresh under cold water, drain again and toss with the rice noodles.

Toss the chicken and about two-thirds of the chopped herbs into the noodles and transfer to a large serving dish. Scatter over the toasted nuts, then the remaining herbs and serve.

# Potato salad with dill
## and pickled red onion

This quick pickling treatment for onion comes from River Cottage Canteen chef, Tim Maddams. He does it with rosemary, but the light sugar-salt-vinegar cure really brings out the flavour of dill too. This creamy, moreish side dish is very good with salmon or trout, whether smoked or cooked and cooled. I also like it with a bit of salty ham.

*Serves 4 as a side dish*

½ fairly small red onion, peeled and finely chopped
A good pinch of caster sugar
2 tsp cider vinegar
2 heaped tbsp chopped dill

300g cold cooked new potatoes, thickly sliced
4 tbsp soured cream
Sea salt and freshly ground black pepper

Put the chopped onion into a bowl. Sprinkle over a good pinch each of salt and sugar and a grinding of pepper. Toss well and leave for 10 minutes to soften. If the onion releases a lot of liquid, drain it off.

Sprinkle over the cider vinegar and chopped dill, stir and then leave to stand for another 10 minutes. Fold in the potatoes and the soured cream, check the seasoning (it may well need a bit more salt) and serve.

# Herb omelette

A simple omelette is not just an almost instant and very delicious lunch, it's also an ideal way to taste and savour any number of different herbs – the perfect quick recipe, in fact, if you're experimenting with something new.

*Herbs to use*
**Chives and/or garlic chives**
***Fines herbes*** **(a blend of tarragon, parsley, chervil and chives)**
**Flat-leaf parsley with a tiny bit of lovage**
**Marjoram**
**Rocket**
**Sorrel**
**Wild garlic**

*Serves 1*
**2 eggs**
**Small knob of unsalted butter**
   **(about 5g)**
**About 1 tbsp chopped or shredded**
   **herbs (see above)**
**Sea salt and freshly ground**
   **black pepper**

Lightly beat the eggs together with some salt and pepper. Heat a 15–20cm frying pan or omelette pan over a medium heat, then add the butter.

As soon as the butter is melted and bubbling, pour in the eggs. Use a fork to lift and push the sides of the omelette as it starts to set, so the liquid egg can run down on to the base of the pan.

After about a minute, scatter the herbs evenly over the omelette. Keep cooking for a minute or so longer, until done to your liking, then fold the omelette in half with a fork or spatula and slide on to a plate. Eat straight away.

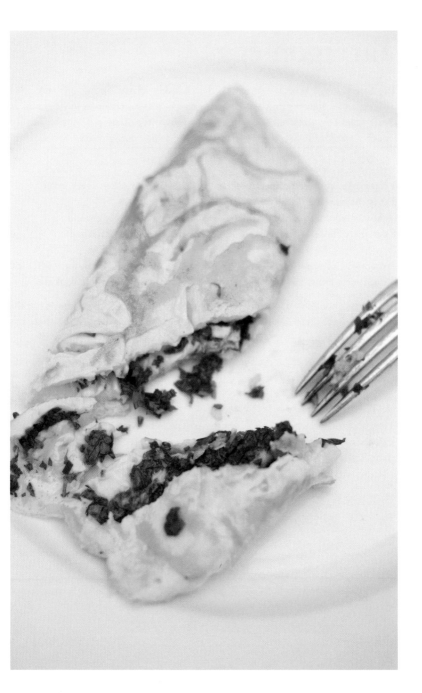

# Tarragon eggs

This simple, slightly retro little dish makes a lovely starter. Tarragon is very good with eggs but, like the previous omelette recipe, this one is open to variation, as the egg and mayonnaise make an excellent vehicle for many different herbs. Try fennel, a pinch of lovage or very finely chopped young borage leaves, for instance.

*Serves 4 as a starter*

4 large eggs, at room temperature
3 tbsp mayonnaise (ideally
    homemade, see p.159)
4 tsp finely chopped tarragon

Little Gem or other sweet, crisp
    lettuce leaves
Sea salt and freshly ground
    black pepper (if needed)

Bring a pan of water to the boil. Add the eggs and simmer them for 9 minutes. Immediately drain and run the eggs under cold water to stop them cooking.

When cool enough to handle, peel the eggs. Halve them lengthways, scoop out the yolks and mash these in a bowl with the mayonnaise and tarragon (you shouldn't need to add seasoning if the mayonnaise is already well seasoned).

Carefully spoon the egg mayonnaise mixture back into the egg hollows. Serve with a few crisp lettuce leaves.

## Variation

If you leave the boiled eggs whole and chop them, whites and all, before combining with the mayonnaise and herbs, you have a lovely topping for a crisp brown bread canapé, or a rather elegant sandwich filling.

# Pasta with sardines and fennel

This is my take on a traditional Sicilian dish. If you object to the tiny bones in sardine fillets, you could use mackerel instead.

*Serves 4*

300g linguine or spaghetti,
　or pasta shapes
4 tbsp olive oil
1 onion, peeled, quartered and
　finely sliced
1 garlic clove, peeled and cut
　into slivers
3–4 tbsp chopped fennel herb

50g sultanas or raisins
50g pine nuts, toasted
2 tsp balsamic vinegar
A few squeezes of lemon juice
8 sardine fillets (or use 4 whole
　sardines, if you prefer)
Sea salt and freshly ground
　black pepper

Bring a large pan of water to the boil, salt it well and then add the pasta. Cook until al dente, using the time suggested on the packet as a guide.

Meanwhile, heat 3 tbsp olive oil in a frying pan over a medium heat. Add the onion with a pinch each of salt and pepper and sweat for about 5 minutes, until soft and golden. Add the garlic, most of the fennel (reserve a little for finishing), the sultanas and pine nuts. Cook for another 2 minutes, then stir in the balsamic vinegar and turn off the heat.

Drain the pasta well and tip it into the frying pan with the onion mixture. Stir, then return the lot to the hot pasta pan, scraping in all the oil and flavourings. Add a squeeze of lemon juice and toss well. Check the seasoning, then cover the pan to keep everything warm.

Cook the sardines quickly: wipe out the frying pan, add another 1 tbsp oil and put over a medium heat. Season the flesh side of the sardine fillets well. Put them, skin side down, in the pan and cook for about 2 minutes, until the flesh is just about all opaque. Flip over and cook for another minute.

Heap the pasta into warmed dishes, top with the sardine fillets, give the whole lot a good squeeze of lemon juice and finish with a sprinkling of fennel.

# Baked white fish
## with a hyssop and orange crust

This is a quick and simple way to make a plain slab of white fish that much more delicious and enticing. I love the slight sourness of hyssop with the juicy sweetness of the fish flesh, but this recipe will also work well with rosemary or lemon thyme, and with lemon instead of orange zest.

*Serves 4*

4 fat fillets of white fish, such
    as pollack, coley or sustainably
    caught cod or haddock, about
    175g each
A little olive oil
Sea salt and freshly ground
    black pepper

*For the crust*

200g fresh white breadcrumbs
    (from good robust bread
    such as sourdough)
1 tbsp finely chopped hyssop
1 large garlic clove, peeled and
    finely chopped
Finely grated zest of 1 large
    or 2 small oranges
2 tbsp olive oil

Preheat the oven to 220°C/Gas mark 7. Lightly oil a baking tray with a shallow lip (you want the fish to be exposed to the heat on all sides, but its juices need to be contained).

For the crust, mix all the ingredients together well and season with salt and pepper. Lightly oil and season the fish fillets and put them on the baking tray. Press the breadcrumb crust all over the fish in a thick, even layer.

Bake for 15 minutes until the crust is golden brown and the fish is cooked through, then serve straight away. This is very nice with roasted cherry tomatoes and roughly crushed potatoes, although green veg would work well too.

# Pork with fennel and rosemary

This is inspired by the traditional Italian dish of *porchetta*, where a whole suckling pig is stuffed and roasted. Aromatic fennel and rosemary are often used to flavour the meat, and they work just as well on a smaller scale. If possible, store the pork uncovered in the fridge for at least 12 hours before cooking. This helps to dry out the rind, resulting in better crackling.

*Serves 4–8*

1–2kg piece of boned-out pork shoulder
2–4 dessert apples (depending on the size of your joint), cored and cut into 6–8 wedges each
About 300ml well-flavoured chicken or vegetable stock
Fine sea salt

*For the flavouring paste*
3 garlic cloves, peeled
2 tsp fennel seeds
2 tbsp chopped rosemary
Finely grated zest of 1 lemon
2–4 tbsp olive oil
Sea salt and freshly ground black pepper

Preheat the oven to 240°C/Gas mark 9. Score the pork rind if it isn't already scored.

For the paste, crush the garlic with a pinch of salt in a mortar. Add the fennel seeds and pound roughly, then work in the rosemary, lemon zest and some pepper. Bind together with the olive oil – just enough to make a coarse spreadable paste.

Open out the pork and lay it skin side down on a board. If it is mostly in one thick piece, use a sharp knife to open up the existing cavity or slice into the thicker parts to create a bigger surface area. Rub the herb paste all over the inside of the meat, working it into every crevice. Roll up the meat as best you can and tie tightly with string in 3 or 4 places. Place, skin side up, in a roasting tin. Wipe any excess oil or stuffing off the skin with kitchen paper. Sprinkle the rind generously with fine salt.

Roast for 20 minutes, then lower the setting to 180°C/Gas mark 4 and roast for a further 35 minutes per 500g, putting the apples around the meat about 30 minutes before the end of cooking. Check that the meat is cooked by piercing the thickest part and pressing the joint; there must be no trace of pink in the juices.

Leave the pork to rest in a warm place for 10–15 minutes before carving. Spoon the rich juices from the dish over the meat as you serve it. Or, to make more of a gravy, take the pork and apples out of the roasting tin, add about 300ml stock to the tin and let it bubble over a medium heat on the hob to reduce while you scrape up the caramelised bits, then pour into a jug. The pork is also very nice cold.

# Beef stew with lovage

Lovage lends a good deep flavour to any stew or soup and in this hearty beef dish its delicately spicy side comes to the fore as well.

*Serves 6–8*

4 tbsp rapeseed or olive oil
2 medium onions, peeled and
    finely sliced
1kg braising steak or other stewing
    beef, cut into cubes
4 medium carrots, peeled and sliced
2 tbsp chopped lovage
150ml red wine

A couple of bay leaves or, even better,
    a bouquet garni (see p.19)
About 300ml beef or chicken stock,
    or water
About 500g potatoes, peeled and
    thickly sliced
Sea salt and freshly ground
    black pepper

Heat 2 tbsp oil in a large flameproof casserole. Add the onions and sweat down for 10 minutes or so.

Meanwhile, heat another 1 tbsp oil in a large frying pan over a fairly high heat. Season half the beef with salt and pepper and add to the hot frying pan. Fry, turning once or twice, until nicely browned all over, then add to the casserole with the onions. Repeat the process to brown the rest of the beef. Add to the casserole with the sliced carrots and half the chopped lovage.

Use the wine to deglaze the frying pan, stirring well to scrape up any caramelised bits, and letting it simmer for a few minutes to reduce a little. Add to the casserole.

Add the bay leaves or bouquet garni and enough stock or water to just barely cover the meat and veg. Bring to a simmer. Cover, turn the heat to very low and cook at a very gentle simmer for an hour.

Add the sliced potatoes, give the stew a stir and cook at a very low simmer for another hour. Stir in the remaining chopped lovage and some salt and pepper and serve with shredded greens and some rice or bread.

# Stuffed breast of lamb
## with dried apricots and winter savory

Breast of lamb is a strange-looking cut of meat, but so delicious and inexpensive. It's made for stuffing and rolling, and the pungent piney note of winter savory enhances it beautifully.

*Serves 2–3*

**1 breast of lamb**
**Sea salt and freshly ground**
   **black pepper**

*For the stuffing*
**1 tbsp rapeseed or olive oil**
**1 small onion, peeled and chopped**
**1 garlic clove, peeled and chopped**
**50g breadcrumbs**
**3 dried apricots, chopped**
**2 tbsp chopped winter savory**
**1 small egg, beaten**

Preheat the oven to 200°C/Gas mark 6.

For the stuffing, heat the oil in a frying pan over a medium heat. Add the onion and garlic and sauté gently for about 10 minutes, until soft. Leave to cool a little, then combine with the breadcrumbs, dried apricots, winter savory, beaten egg and some seasoning.

Unroll the breast of lamb, season the surface with salt and pepper, and spread the stuffing over it. Roll up again and secure with cocktail sticks or string. Roast for 30 minutes, then lower the oven setting to 150°C/Gas mark 2 and cook for a further 1½ hours.

Leave the lamb to rest in a warm place for 15 minutes, then slice it thickly. As this cut of lamb is rich and quite fatty, you only need some simply cooked vegetables with it – perhaps boiled or mashed potatoes and some steamed greens, sauced with a lick of the rich juices from the tin.

# Loin of lamb with lavender
## and lemon thyme

I'm certainly not the first person to think of roasting lamb with lavender, but this is my particular take on the idea. The lemon thyme seems to work so well, really enhancing the floral qualities of the lavender. If you don't have any, you could use ordinary thyme.

*Serves 4*

2 tbsp finely chopped lavender leaves
2 tsp finely chopped lemon thyme
Finely grated zest of 1 lemon
1 fat garlic clove, peeled and
    finely chopped
About 2 tbsp rapeseed or olive oil

500–600g piece of boned-out
    lamb loin
A little white wine or stock,
    for deglazing (optional)
Sea salt and freshly ground
    black pepper

Preheat the oven to 220°C/Gas mark 7.

Combine the lavender, lemon thyme, lemon zest and garlic in a small bowl. Add some seasoning and just enough oil to make a thick paste.

Lay the meat, skin side down, on a board and smear the herb mixture all over the inside surface, working it into all the cracks and crevices. Fold the meat over on itself and tie securely in several places with string. Smear any escaping oil over the outside and season with salt and pepper.

Place the meat in a roasting dish, with the 'open' edge uppermost to keep the flavouring mix inside. Roast for 15 minutes, then lower the oven setting to 170°C/ Gas mark 3 and roast for a further 15 minutes for just-pink lamb.

Leave the lamb to rest in a warm place for 15 minutes before slicing. Deglaze the pan with a little white wine or stock, or even a splash of water, to create a few spoonfuls of flavoursome gravy.

# Baked chicken
## with forty cloves of garlic

This is an incredibly simple and delicious dish. It's worth making it to feed three or four, then using the leftovers over the next few days. The garlic-infused chicken is wonderful cold in sandwiches, or chopped up and reheated in its rich oily juices then combined with waxy potatoes and peas or beans. Choose a good, but not too overpowering, olive oil – its flavour will be significant in the finished dish.

*Serves 6–8*

1 chicken, about 1.8kg, jointed
    into 8 pieces
100ml extra virgin olive oil
A few sprigs of rosemary
A couple of bay leaves
4 garlic bulbs, broken into
    individual cloves (unpeeled)

½ glass of white wine (optional)
Juice of ½ lemon
Sea salt and freshly ground
    black pepper

Preheat the oven to 180°C/Gas mark 4.

Season the chicken pieces well all over with salt and pepper. Heat 2–3 tbsp of the extra virgin olive oil in a large non-stick frying pan over a medium-high heat and sear the chicken all over. You'll probably have to do this in two batches. Transfer the chicken pieces to an oven dish, placing them skin side up.

Tuck the rosemary and bay leaves around the chicken pieces, then scatter over the unpeeled garlic cloves, pushing them down so they nestle low in the pan, between the chicken pieces.

Deglaze the browning pan with the wine (or use water), stirring well to scrape up any bits of caramelised chicken. Pour this into the tin (not over the chicken skin). Squeeze over the lemon juice, trickle over the remaining olive oil and scatter extra salt and pepper on the chicken skin.

Cover the dish with foil and bake for 30 minutes, then uncover, turn the oven up to 190°C/Gas mark 5 and bake for a further 20 minutes, or until the chicken pieces are well browned and cooked through.

Serve with something that will soak up the abundant oily juices – new potatoes, mash, rice or good bread – and a green vegetable or salad, such as watercress.

# Roast chicken with
## lemon and myrtle

The bay-and-orange scent of myrtle informs this dish in a wonderfully subtle way. You could replace it with another woody herb: thyme, rosemary, summer savory and marjoram all spring to mind, or a combination of two or three of these.

*Serves 4, with leftovers*

1 chicken, about 1.75–2kg
2 large sprigs of myrtle, each
   with 15–20 leaves
1 lemon
1 small garlic clove, peeled

100g unsalted butter, softened
A small glass of dry white wine
   (optional)
Sea salt and freshly ground
   black pepper

Take the chicken out of the fridge about an hour before cooking so it comes up to room temperature. Preheat the oven to 220°C/Gas mark 7.

Take the leaves from 1 myrtle sprig and chop them roughly. Put in a mortar. Grate the zest from the lemon and add this, with the garlic and a good pinch each of salt and pepper. Crush to a rough paste, then combine with the softened butter.

Untruss the chicken and put it in a roasting dish. Pull the legs away from the body slightly so hot air can circulate. Pack as much of the flavoured butter as you can under the skin of the breast, smoothing it along without tearing the skin. Smear any remaining butter over the outside of the bird. Put two quarters of the derinded lemon inside the bird. Bash the remaining myrtle sprig to crush the leaves a little and add to the cavity too. Season the skin and the cavity with more salt and pepper.

Roast the chicken for 20 minutes. Remove the roasting tin from the oven and pour the wine (or just use water) into the tin (not over the bird). Lower the oven setting to 180°C/Gas mark 4 and roast the chicken for a further 40 minutes.

Turn the oven off, prop the door open slightly and leave the chicken inside to rest and finish cooking for 15 minutes. Check that it is cooked by plunging a skewer into the thickest part of the meat, where the leg joins the body. Press with a spoon; the juices that run out should be clear. If they are pink, the chicken is not cooked.

Carve the chicken and serve with its delicious buttery juices – all the gravy you'll need. This requires nothing more than some bread and a crisp salad, but potatoes and other veg – particularly wilted shredded greens or kale – would be good too.

# Spring pasta with wild garlic
## and purple sprouting broccoli

If you're not lucky enough to have a source of wild garlic, you can use a freshly snipped bunch of chives or, even better, garlic chives here. Very finely sliced Welsh onion tops would be good too. And, of course, you could use ordinary broccoli instead of purple sprouting.

*Serves 2*

175g pasta shapes of your choice
150g purple sprouting broccoli (or ordinary broccoli), chopped into small pieces
A knob of unsalted butter
50g soft rindless goat's cheese

4–6 wild garlic leaves, finely shredded
A little extra virgin olive oil
Sea salt and freshly ground black pepper
Finely grated Parmesan or hard goat's cheese, to serve

Bring a large pan of water to the boil, salt it well and then add the pasta. Cook until al dente, using the time suggested on the packet as a guide, adding the broccoli to the pan about 5 minutes before the pasta will be done.

Drain the pasta and broccoli and, while still piping hot, add the butter and goat's cheese, letting them melt and coat the pasta and veg. Season with salt and pepper to taste, then fold in the wild garlic.

Serve straight away in warmed bowls. Top with a trickle of good extra virgin olive oil and a scattering of Parmesan or hard goat's cheese.

# Aubergines with perilla

The slightly cumin-like flavour of perilla is lovely with aubergines. You could use the green or the purple variety here, though the purple looks particularly striking. This is delicious with some warm flatbreads and a scoop of soft goat's cheese or some garlicky yoghurt.

*Serves 4 as a starter or side dish*
2 medium aubergines, thinly sliced
Olive oil for brushing
12 spring onions, halved lengthways
About 12 perilla leaves, chopped
Sea salt and freshly ground
    black pepper

*For the dressing*
3 tbsp olive oil
A good squirt of lemon juice
½ tsp thin honey

Sprinkle the aubergine slices with salt and leave in a colander for 30 minutes or so to draw out the juices. Rinse the aubergines quickly and pat dry with kitchen paper.

For the dressing, mix the olive oil, lemon juice and honey together and season well with salt and pepper.

Brush the aubergines with olive oil and sear in a hot pan for a couple of minutes each side, until tender and golden. Do the same thing with the spring onions.

Layer the hot veg in a dish, trickling a little dressing and scattering some of the perilla over each layer. Leave until just warm, or completely cold, then serve.

# Runner beans
## with summer savory

This is good served alongside anything from a simple potato and onion frittata to barbecued sausages. It works well with herbs other than summer savory – try tarragon, lemon thyme, marjoram or anise hyssop. You could use French beans too; these will need a little less cooking.

*Serves 4 as a side dish*

500g runner beans
2 tbsp rapeseed or olive oil
3–4 shallots or 1 small onion, peeled and finely chopped
1 small garlic clove, peeled and finely chopped

1 tbsp finely chopped summer savory
Sea salt and freshly ground black pepper

Use a potato peeler to remove the stringy fibres from the edges of the runner beans, top and tail them, then cut into 1–2cm pieces.

Heat the oil in a wide saucepan over a medium heat. Add the shallots or onion and sweat down for about 10 minutes, until soft. Add the garlic and beans. Cover the pan, lower the heat and sweat for another 10 minutes.

Add about 150ml water and continue to cook, uncovered, for a further 10–15 minutes, stirring from time to time. You want the beans to be just tender but still with a bit of crunch. Add the savory a couple of minutes before the end of cooking. Season with salt and pepper to taste and serve.

# White beans with winter herbs

Baked beans, but not as you know them... This simple, pleasingly rustic dish is inspired by a Simon Hopkinson recipe. It is a doddle to do, very economical and fabulous comfort food.

*Serves 4*

250g dried white beans, such as cannellini, soaked for several hours in cold water
1–2 bay leaves, twisted
1 large sprig of rosemary
1 large sprig of winter savory or sage
2–3 garlic cloves (unpeeled), roughly squashed
500ml lamb or chicken stock
Sea salt and freshly ground black pepper

*To finish*
A little olive oil
100g diced pancetta or bacon lardons
1 garlic clove, peeled and finely chopped
1 tsp finely chopped rosemary
Extra virgin olive or rapeseed oil

Preheat your oven to 160°C/Gas mark 3.

Drain and rinse the soaked beans and put them into a casserole dish. Add the herbs, garlic cloves and stock. (I usually tie up the herbs in a square of muslin to stop the leaves straying throughout the dish, but this isn't essential.) Bring to the boil on the hob, then cover and transfer to the oven. Bake for 1–2 hours, until the beans are beautifully tender. Fish out the herbs and garlic.

To finish, heat a splash of olive oil in a frying pan and fry the bacon or pancetta for a few minutes, until just turning crisp. Add the chopped garlic and rosemary and immediately turn off the heat. Stir them into the bacon so the residual heat mellows the garlic, just a touch.

Season the beans with salt and pepper to taste. Ladle into deep dishes, scatter the bacon mixture over the top and finish with a swirl of virgin oil. Serve with bread.

# Double fennel braise

I have a passion for fennel – the herb and the vegetable – so I'm very fond of this dish. It makes a lovely accompaniment to fish but is also very good simply tossed into pasta and finished with some Parmesan.

*Serves 4*

1 tbsp olive or rapeseed oil
4 fat bulbs of Florence fennel, tough
    outer layers removed, cut into
    8 wedges each, intact at the core
About 200ml chicken or
    vegetable stock

1 fat garlic clove
2 tbsp finely chopped fennel herb
Sea salt and freshly ground
    black pepper

Preheat the oven to 180°C/Gas mark 4.

Heat the oil in a large frying pan over a medium-high heat. Add the fennel wedges and sear for about 10 minutes, turning once or twice, until they are caramelised on both sides. Transfer to an oven dish.

Deglaze the frying pan with the stock, letting it fizz and simmer for a minute, then pour over the fennel in the dish. Add a good sprinkling of salt and pepper and transfer to the oven. Braise for 20 minutes, or until the fennel is tender.

Meanwhile, finely chop the garlic and combine with the chopped fennel herb. Once the braised fennel is ready, immediately stir in the herb mix, so the heat of the fennel just softens the raw garlic. Serve straight away.

# Creamed Swiss chard

This recipe is closely based on one I came across in a lovely American cookbook, *With A Measure of Grace*, written by the owners of a Buddhist restaurant in Utah. It travels well. This is a rich and comforting side dish and a little goes a long way – try it with roast chicken, or simply cooked Puy lentils.

*Serves 4–6*

A large knob of unsalted butter
1 onion, peeled and finely chopped
1 garlic clove, peeled and finely chopped
350g Swiss chard leaves, including the tender parts of the stems, shredded

250ml double cream
20g Parmesan, grated
35g fresh breadcrumbs
1 heaped tbsp finely chopped tarragon
Sea salt and freshly ground black pepper

Heat the butter in a large saucepan over a medium-low heat. Add the onion and sweat down gently for about 10 minutes until softened. Add the garlic and cook for a few more minutes.

Add the shredded chard, cream, Parmesan, breadcrumbs, chopped tarragon and some salt and pepper. Keep the heat low and cook gently, stirring often, for about 10 minutes or until you have a rich, thick mixture. Check the seasoning and serve.

# Rosemary focaccia

Serve this shallow Italian bread still warm and fragrant from the oven, ready to be torn into chunks and dipped into soup, stew or just a bit more olive oil. The dough is very loose and sticky. Persevere with it if you can: the wet consistency ensures the relaxed form and lovely open texture of a really good focaccia. If you're new to kneading, or you just don't feel very confident, you can either start off with a touch less water – try 325ml – or add generous amounts of flour while you knead. Your bread will still be good. Alternatively, use a mixer with a dough hook.

*Serves 6–8*

500g strong white bread flour
1 tsp easy-blend yeast
10g fine sea salt
3 tbsp extra virgin olive oil, plus
    extra to finish

1 tbsp chopped rosemary
Coarse sea salt, to finish

Put the flour, yeast and salt into a large bowl and mix well. Add the 3 tbsp extra virgin olive oil and 350ml warm water. Mix to a rough dough. Turn out on to a floured surface and knead for about 5 minutes, adding extra flour only if you need to. My technique is to slap the dough down, then use the heel of one hand to push it away from me, stretching it out, then scoop it back over itself and repeat. It will stick to your hands but it's worth it.

Oil your hands generously with more olive oil and scoop up the kneaded dough, oiling it all over as you do so. Put in a clean bowl, cover with cling film and leave to rise in a warm place until doubled in size (at least an hour, up to two).

Brush a shallow-sided baking tray, about 22 x 30cm, with olive oil. Tip the dough out on to a floured work surface. Without 'knocking it back' first, flatten into a rough rectangle, then transfer to the oiled baking tray. Push the dough out to fill the tray in an even layer. Cover again and leave until puffy and increased in size by about half (at least 30 minutes). Meanwhile, heat your oven to 220°C/Gas mark 7.

Use a fingertip to push deep dimples all over the dough. Scatter with the chopped rosemary and some coarse salt, then trickle generously with more olive oil. Bake for 10 minutes, then reduce the heat to 180°C/Gas mark 4 and bake for a further 10 minutes, until golden.

Allow to cool a little, but serve still warm. Focaccia is best eaten soon after baking. If it's gone cold, reheat it gently before serving.

# Fennel seed bread

This well-flavoured loaf is great with cheese or salty air-dried ham. You can replace some of the fennel seeds with celery seeds for a subtly different flavour.

*Makes 1 loaf*

| | |
|---|---|
| 2 tbsp fennel seeds | 1 tsp easy-blend yeast |
| 500g strong white flour | 2 tbsp thin honey |
| 10g fine sea salt | 1 tbsp olive oil |

Lightly toast the fennel seeds in a dry frying pan for a few minutes, until fragrant. Transfer to a mortar and roughly crush with the pestle.

Combine the crushed seeds with the flour, salt and yeast. Measure the honey into a measuring jug and make up to 325ml with warm water. Add to the flour with the olive oil and mix to a rough dough.

Turn out on to a clean surface and knead for 5–10 minutes. It will be quite a sticky dough, which is as it should be – you get better bread this way. You can add a little more flour to help you knead if you like, but don't overdo it. Alternatively, smear a little more olive oil on your work surface and hands to stop the dough sticking.

Shape the kneaded dough into a smooth round, coat with a little olive oil and place in a large clean bowl. Cover with cling film and leave to rise in a warm place until doubled in size – at least an hour, up to two.

Tip the risen dough out on to a lightly floured surface and deflate it with your fingertips. Shape again into a neat round, or a short, fat baguette if you prefer. Place on an oiled baking sheet. Alternatively, use a proving basket, if you have one. Cover lightly with a tea towel and leave until roughly doubled in size again (about an hour).

Preheat your oven to its highest setting. Cut a couple of slashes in the top of the loaf with a sharp knife or a baker's razor blade (a lame), or make deep snips with scissors. Bake at maximum temperature for 10 minutes, then reduce the setting to 180°C/Gas mark 4 and bake for a further 20 minutes, or until the loaf is golden brown and sounds hollow when tapped underneath. Transfer to a wire rack and leave to cool completely before slicing.

# Soda bread with rosemary
## and sultanas

Soda bread is quick, easy and just as delicious as freshly baked yeasted bread. You can doctor your homemade soda breads with various additions, including fresh herbs – woody, pungent ones, such as thyme and rosemary, work best. This particular incarnation is a quick-to-make homage to the divine rosemary and raisin bread made at Sally Clarke's bakery in London. It's lovely with soup or a salad, or just spread with salty butter – as is the cheesy thyme variation below.

*Makes 1 large loaf*

500g plain white or refined spelt flour
1 tsp fine sea salt
1 tsp bicarbonate of soda
1 tbsp finely chopped rosemary

150g sultanas
300ml plain full-fat yoghurt
200ml whole milk

Preheat the oven to 200°C/Gas mark 6. Lightly oil a baking sheet or line one with baking parchment.

Sift the flour, salt and bicarbonate of soda together into a bowl. Stir in the chopped rosemary and sultanas. Make a well in the middle.

Whisk the yoghurt and milk together until smooth. Add to the dry ingredients and mix until just combined. This will give you a soft, sticky dough, which is how I like it, as it makes a nice moist loaf.

With floured hands, or a spatula, scrape the dough on to the prepared baking sheet and pat it into a rough round. Bake for 45 minutes until risen and golden brown.

Leave the bread to cool on a wire rack. Eat as it is within 24 hours or, if you've left it longer than that, toast the slices. The loaf freezes well too.

## Variation

**Soda bread with thyme, Cheddar and mustard**  Use 250g spelt or wholemeal flour mixed with 250g plain white flour. Replace the rosemary and sultanas with 100g grated strong Cheddar and 1 tbsp finely chopped thyme. Whisk 2 tsp English mustard into the yoghurt and milk before combining with the dry ingredients.

# Bergamot scones

The subtle herby flavour of these savoury scones makes them delicious alongside a bowl of soup, but I like to eat them on their own too – warm from the oven, with just a smear of salty butter. They are also good made with thyme or marjoram.

*Makes 8*

250g self-raising white flour
¼ tsp salt
50g cold unsalted butter, diced
1 good tbsp finely chopped bergamot

35g Parmesan, finely grated
175ml whole milk, plus extra
  for glazing

Preheat the oven to 220°C/Gas mark 7 and grease a baking tray.

Sift the flour and salt into a bowl. Add the butter and rub in with your fingertips until thoroughly incorporated. Alternatively, do this in a food processor, then tip into a mixing bowl. Stir in the bergamot and Parmesan. Mix in the milk to form a soft, slightly sticky dough, but don't overwork it.

Tip the dough out on to a floured surface, knead lightly, then pat or roll to a rough circle 2.5–3cm thick. Cut into 8 triangles. Transfer to the baking sheet and brush each scone with milk. Bake for about 12 minutes, until risen and golden. Eat these scones on the day you make them, ideally still warm, or freeze.

# Minted red berry sorbet

The mintiness of this gorgeous deep-pink sorbet makes it especially refreshing. Mint also has a seasoning effect on many fruits, and really enhances the raspberry and strawberry flavours here. Make sure you use spearmint rather than the more pungent peppermint (see p.105).

*Serves 4*

115g caster sugar
2 large leafy stems of spearmint,
     plus 2 tbsp finely chopped
     spearmint leaves to finish
500g mixed raspberries and
     strawberries, roughly half and half

Put the sugar into a saucepan with 200ml water. Heat gently, stirring often, until the sugar has dissolved. Increase the heat. Once simmering, cook the sugar syrup for 5 minutes. Turn off the heat. Roughly bruise the stems of mint and add these to the hot syrup, pushing them under the surface. Leave to cool completely.

Crush the berries roughly with your hands or a potato masher to get the juices flowing, then transfer to a blender and blitz to a purée. Work the purée through a sieve to remove all the pips.

Strain the cooled minty syrup into the berry purée, pressing the mint with a spoon to extract every last drop of flavour. Stir in the finely chopped mint leaves, then chill in the fridge.

Once cold, churn in an ice-cream maker until just set, then transfer to a suitable container and freeze until solid. (If you don't have an ice-cream maker, freeze in a shallow container, beating with a fork at hourly intervals until the sorbet is solid.)

Transfer the sorbet to the fridge 30 minutes or so before serving to soften. Serve scooped into small dishes.

Raspberry ripple basil ice cream

# Herb ice cream or custard

A classic custard, or *crème anglaise*, subtly infused with the scent and flavour of one well-chosen herb can be a heady delight. And, of course, it can form the base for a delectable homemade herb ice cream. A frozen custard, however, needs to be sweeter than a chilled one, so use 100g sugar if making ice cream rather than 50g.

If you're making the custard, serve it chilled with lightly sugared strawberries or raspberries, or baked sweetened rhubarb, poached pears, a gooseberry compote, or roasted peaches or plums.

Herbs to use
**Bay leaves** Use 4–6 leaves, each torn into 2–3 pieces
**Lavender** Use 2 tbsp chopped leaves and/or flowers
**Lemon verbena** Use 8–12 roughly chopped leaves
**Basil** Use 1 bunch (about 40g), stalks and leaves roughly torn or chopped

*Makes about 600ml*

**200ml double cream**
**300ml whole milk**
**Your choice of herb (see above)**

**4 large egg yolks**
**50–100g caster sugar (see above)**

Put the cream, milk and chosen herb into a saucepan. Bring to just below boiling point, then remove from the heat and set aside to infuse for about 1 hour.

Whisk the egg yolks and sugar together in a bowl (use 50g sugar for a custard, 100g for an ice cream). Strain the cream mixture into a jug, pressing the herbs with a spoon to extract all the flavour. Pour on to the yolks and sugar, whisking all the time. Pour the mixture into a clean saucepan. Heat gently, stirring all the time, until the custard thickens; don't let it boil, or it will curdle. Remove from the heat and cover the surface with cling film to stop a skin forming.

Once cool, your custard can be chilled, ready to serve. Alternatively, for a fragrant ice, churn the sweeter custard in an ice-cream maker, then put into the freezer.

## Variation

Raspberry ripple basil ice cream For the ripple, put 300g raspberries, 30g caster sugar and 2 tbsp water into a pan. Bring to the boil and simmer for a few minutes. Press through a sieve back into the pan and boil for 5–10 minutes until thick. Cool and chill. Make a basil custard and churn until thick. Marble the raspberry sauce through the semi-set ice cream before putting in the freezer.

# Lemon verbena layer
## with raspberries

This is a very simple way to showcase the lovely citrus tang of lemon verbena, which goes perfectly with raspberries. You could use strawberries instead if you like, or a sweetened blackcurrant purée.

*Serves 4*

100g digestive or shortbread biscuits, crushed to rough crumbs
2 tsp finely chopped lemon verbena, plus 4 little sprigs, to garnish
50g caster sugar

100g full-fat fromage frais
100ml double cream
1 large egg white
300g raspberries
Icing sugar, to serve

Divide the biscuit crumbs between 4 glass tumblers or sundae dishes.

Using a pestle and mortar, grind and pound the chopped lemon verbena with half the sugar until you have a fine, pale green sugar with no significant pieces of lemon verbena leaf visible.

Mix the verbena sugar with the fromage frais and cream in a large bowl. If the mixture is not already thick (this depends on the texture of the fromage frais to start with), beat until it forms soft peaks.

Beat the egg white until it holds stiff peaks. Add the remaining sugar and beat again until you have a glossy meringue that holds firm peaks. Fold this lightly into the fromage frais mixture. Spoon over the biscuits in the glasses.

Top with the raspberries and chill for an hour or so. Just before serving, add the sprigs of lemon verbena and a dusting of icing sugar.

# Rhubarb crumble
## with angelica

Tender angelica stalk is just wonderful combined with rhubarb, lifting its flavour and softening its acidity. The fresh green seeds of sweet cicely have a very similar effect. You can use your favourite crumble topping here, or mine.

*Serves 4–6*

750g rhubarb, trimmed and chopped
50ml apple or orange juice
1 tbsp finely chopped young angelica
    stem (or finely chopped young
    green sweet cicely pods)
50g caster sugar

*For the crumble topping*
150g plain flour
150g fine oatmeal
A pinch of fine sea salt
125g cold unsalted butter, cubed
85g demerara sugar

Preheat the oven to 180°C/Gas mark 4.

To make the topping, put the flour, oatmeal and salt in a food processor. Add the butter and pulse just until combined. Tip the mixture out into a bowl and stir in the demerara sugar.

Put the rhubarb into a 20cm square oven dish (or similar). Sprinkle over the apple or orange juice and the angelica. Toss together lightly, then sprinkle the sugar evenly over. Put into the oven for about 20 minutes to soften the fruit.

Give the fruit a stir and pat it down into a fairly flat, even layer. Squeeze handfuls of the topping together in your hands, then crumble them over the fruit so you get a lumpy, crumbly mix. Bake for 30 minutes, until the crumble is golden brown and the fruit is bubbling underneath. Serve with cream or ice cream.

# Lemon and lavender biscuits

These delicate buttery biscuits are perfect with an afternoon cup of tea (or some late-night ice cream). For a quite different result, replace the lavender with 1 tsp lightly toasted and roughly crushed caraway seeds.

*Makes about 25*

125g unsalted butter, softened
75g caster sugar, plus a little extra
  for dredging
1 tbsp finely chopped fresh lavender
  leaves and/or flowers

Finely grated zest of 1 lemon
100g plain flour
100g cornflour
A pinch of fine sea salt

Beat the butter, sugar, lavender and lemon zest together briefly in a large bowl, just until well combined. Sift the flour, cornflour and salt together over the butter and sugar mixture. Use a fork to bring the mixture together into a soft dough. Knead it very briefly in the bowl. Pat into a flat disc, wrap in cling film and refrigerate for 30 minutes.

Preheat the oven to 180°C/Gas mark 4. Line one or two baking sheets with baking parchment or a non-stick liner.

Roll out the dough to a 3–4mm thickness: it's a fairly sticky dough so flour the surface well, or you might find it easier to roll it out on a sheet of baking parchment. Cut out discs using a 6cm cookie cutter and place on the baking sheet(s). Gather the trimmings, re-roll and keep cutting until the dough is all used up.

Bake for about 10 minutes, or until the biscuits are just turning golden at the edges. If you have only one baking sheet, you'll need to bake them in batches.

Leave to cool a little to allow the biscuits to firm up slightly, then carefully transfer to a wire rack. Dredge with a little more caster sugar and leave to cool completely. Store in an airtight tin and eat within a few days.

# Minty chocolate fridge cake

This is one of the nicest combinations of chocolate and mint I've ever tried – using fresh peppermint, rather than a bottled essence, seems to make the mix more fragrant and less pungent. You can cut it into smaller pieces than I suggest here if you like, for a very pleasing petit four.

*Makes 12 pieces*

100g unsalted butter
1 tbsp golden syrup
2 large stems of peppermint, roughly bruised, plus 1 tbsp finely chopped leaves
150g dark chocolate, broken into pieces

100g raisins
75g skinned hazelnuts
75g digestive, shortbread or oaty biscuits, broken into small chunks

Line a loaf tin, about 20 x 10cm, with baking parchment.

Put the butter, golden syrup and bruised peppermint stems into a small pan and heat gently until the butter melts, stirring and crushing the peppermint as you do so. Leave to infuse for half an hour or so, then reheat gently to re-melt the butter.

Put the chocolate into a bowl and strain the minty butter through a sieve on to it, pressing the mint with a spoon to extract every last drop of flavour. Put the bowl of chocolate and butter inside a larger bowl filled with just-boiled water and leave to melt, stirring from time to time.

Meanwhile, combine the raisins, hazelnuts, broken biscuits and chopped mint in a large bowl. When the chocolate and butter mixture is completely melted and smooth, pour it over the raisin mixture and mix thoroughly. Tip into the prepared tin and spread out as evenly as possible. Leave to cool, then refrigerate until firm.

Leave for at least 24 hours to allow the flavours to develop, then lift the cake out of the tin and cut into 12 pieces. Store in an airtight container in the fridge and eat within a week.

# White chocolate truffles
## with basil

These are fabulously indulgent and lovely with a cup of coffee. The sweet richness of white chocolate is nicely cut by basil's delicate aniseed flavour.

*Makes about 15*

100ml double cream

25g bunch of basil (stalks and leaves), roughly chopped

200g white chocolate, broken into small pieces

Cocoa powder for dusting OR 100g dark chocolate, broken into small pieces, for coating

Put the cream and basil into a small saucepan. Bring to just below boiling point, stirring and crushing the basil a little, then take off the heat and leave to infuse until cool.

Slowly melt the white chocolate in a bowl set inside a larger bowl filled with just-boiled water. Allow to cool slightly. Strain the basil-infused cream through a sieve on to the melted chocolate, pressing the basil leaves to extract every last drop of flavour. Stir until smooth; the mixture will thicken slightly and darken in colour. Leave to cool completely, then chill for several hours until set firm.

Scoop out teaspoonfuls of the chilled truffle mixture and roll quickly between the palms of your hands to form balls (it's a very sticky mix). You could also, if you're adept, use two teaspoons to form the mix into quenelles. You can now either roll the truffles in cocoa powder and return to the fridge, or coat them in chocolate.

For chocolate-coated truffles, put the truffles in the freezer while you melt the dark chocolate in a bowl set inside a larger bowl filled with just-boiled water. Leave the melted chocolate to cool until thickened and barely warm. Now use a spoon and fork to quickly coat the semi-frozen truffles in the chocolate. Drain each one briefly on the fork then place on a board lined with baking parchment to set before transferring to the fridge.

Keep the truffles in an airtight container in the fridge and eat within a few days.

# Fennel fudge

This utterly moreish sweetmeat is delectably crumbly and melt-in-the-mouth. It can also be made with caraway seeds, although these are best given a good pounding with the pestle and mortar, or a whiz in a spice grinder to break them down a bit as they can be quite tough. Don't reduce them to a powder though – the fudge needs a bit of seedy texture.

*Makes at least 25 pieces*

A few drops of sunflower oil
300g caster sugar
1 tbsp golden syrup
100g unsalted butter, cut into chunks

100ml double cream
1 tbsp fennel seeds
A large pinch of fine sea salt

Put a few drops of sunflower oil on a piece of kitchen paper and use to lightly grease a baking dish, about 20cm square.

Put the sugar, golden syrup, butter and cream into a heavy-based, deep saucepan, making sure the pan is no more than one-third full, as the fudge mixture will bubble up. Heat gently, stirring often, until the butter is melted and the sugar has fully dissolved.

Stop stirring, put a sugar thermometer into the pan and turn up the heat. Bring to the boil and boil until the mixture registers 116°C on the thermometer. Take the pan off the heat and leave to stand for 10 minutes.

Meanwhile, roughly crush the fennel seeds, using a pestle and mortar. Add the fennel seeds to the fudge mixture with the salt and beat vigorously with a wooden spoon until it thickens, loses its gloss, becomes slightly grainy and starts to come away from the base of the pan. This should only take a minute or two of beating, but it can sometimes take longer.

Tip the hot fudge into the greased dish, smooth out and leave to set. Mark the fudge into squares with a small sharp knife as soon as it has set enough to hold the cut. Leave for 3–4 hours to set completely, then remove from the dish.

Store the fudge in an airtight container and use within a couple of weeks.

# Apple herb jelly

You can use various herbs to produce pretty, fragrant jellies. For best results, choose from the more pungent, penetrating varieties, such as those listed below. If you use lemon juice to add the required acidity, the jelly will be relatively light and sweet, and you can use it rather like a fruit jam. If you use vinegar, you will get a slightly more assertive sweet-sour finish, which is ideal if you want to use the jelly alongside savoury dishes – sage jelly with pork, for instance, or mint jelly with lamb. In order to get the chopped herbs suspended evenly throughout the jelly, it's important to leave it to cool slightly before potting.

*Herbs to use*
**Mint** Use vinegar for acidity. Mint jelly is perfect with roast lamb, of course.
**Sage** Use vinegar for acidity. Sage jelly is great with pork.
**Rosemary** Use vinegar for a jelly that is good with almost any roast meat.
**Thyme** Use vinegar. Thyme jelly is lovely with goat's cheese and fresh bread.
**Lemon verbena** Use lemon juice for a nice sweet jelly.
**Lavender** Use lemon juice. Lavender jelly is lovely on scones with cream.

*Makes 6–8 medium jam jars*
**2kg cooking apples, such as Bramley**
**3–4 large leafy stems of your chosen**
    **herb, plus about 4 tbsp finely**
    **chopped herb**
**About 1.5kg granulated sugar**
**About 4 lemons OR 200ml cider vinegar**
    **or white wine vinegar (see above)**

Quarter the apples – cores, skin and all – and thickly slice each quarter. Put the apples into a preserving pan. Roughly bruise, twist or tear the whole stems of herb and add these too. Pour in enough water to just cover the apples. Bring to the boil, then lower the heat and simmer until the apples are completely soft – probably about 15 minutes, but it depends on the apples. You can give the fruit a stir, but avoid crushing or mashing it.

Ladle the apples, herb stems and juices into a jelly bag suspended over a large bowl and leave to drip overnight or at least for several hours. Don't squeeze the jelly bag.

Measure the strained juice. For every 500ml juice, you will need 390g sugar, the strained juice of 1 lemon or 50ml vinegar, and 1 tbsp chopped herbs.

Put a saucer in the fridge to chill. Put the apple juice, sugar and strained lemon juice or vinegar into the cleaned preserving pan. Heat, stirring often, until the sugar is completely dissolved, then bring to a rolling boil. Start checking for setting point after 8 minutes of boiling. Turn off the heat under the jelly while you do so.

To test for a set, drip a little of the jelly on to the cold saucer and return to the fridge for a minute. Push the jelly with your fingertip. If it has formed a significant skin that wrinkles with the push, setting point has been reached. If it hasn't, turn on the heat and boil the jelly for another 2–3 minutes before testing again. If you are unsure, always err on the side of caution here; a lightly set jelly is far nicer to use and eat than a solid one.

Once setting point is reached, turn off the heat and stir in the chopped herbs. Leave the jelly to cool for about 10 minutes, stirring once or twice to help distribute the herbs. Watch carefully and you will be able to observe the point when they are suspended throughout the hot jelly, rather than all floating on top. Pour the jelly slowly and carefully into hot sterilised jars. Seal straight away. Label when cool, then store in a cool, dark place and use within a year. Refrigerate after opening.

# Rose petal jelly

For a pretty pink jelly, you need red rose petals, but this is worth making with any heavily fragranced petals, whatever their colour. Avoid petals that may have been sprayed (see p.121). This is lovely spooned delicately on to freshly baked scones.

*Makes 3–4 medium jam jars*
**500ml loosely packed rose petals
(about 6 blooms)
Juice of 1 lemon
500g jam sugar with pectin**

Put the rose petals into a pan with 500ml water. Bring to a simmer and cook gently for 5 minutes. Leave to cool completely, then strain into a clean pan, crushing out every last drop from the petals with the back of a spoon.

Put a saucer into the fridge to chill. Add the lemon juice and sugar to the rose petal liquid. Heat slowly, stirring, until the sugar has dissolved, then bring to a rolling boil. Allow to boil steadily for 4 minutes, then turn off the heat under the jelly while you test for setting point.

Drip a little of the jelly on to the cold saucer and leave for a minute. Push the jelly with your fingertip. If it has formed a significant skin that wrinkles with the push, setting point has been reached. If it hasn't, turn on the heat and boil the jelly for another minute before testing again. If unsure, always err on the side of caution; a lightly set jelly is far nicer to use and eat than a tough, solid one.

Pour the hot jelly into hot sterilised jars and seal immediately. Label when the jars are completely cool. Store in a cool, dry place and use within a year. Once opened, store in the fridge.

# Candied angelica

These sweet, intensely flavoured fragments can be used as a decoration, but they are more interesting chopped and added to fruit cakes, or simply nibbled as a sweet treat after a meal. The candying process also gives you an angelica-flavoured syrup, which can be added to a fruit salad, or combined with fruit such as cooking apples or rhubarb before cooking. For candying, ideally you need angelica stems that are at least 2cm in diameter but still have a bit of bend in them. Hard, woody stems just won't work.

**About 200g angelica stems**
**About 200g caster sugar**

Cut the angelica stems into short lengths. Put them into a saucepan, cover with water and bring to the boil. Lower the heat and simmer until the stems are tender. This could take as little as 5 or as long as 20 minutes. Drain.

Use a small, sharp knife to peel away the tough fibres on the outside of each stem. Weigh the peeled angelica stems and put them into a container in which they will fit in one layer. Add the same weight of caster sugar and toss the lot together. Leave for 1–2 days until the sugar has formed a rich syrup.

Pour off the syrup into a pan, bring to the boil and simmer for 1 minute, then pour back over the angelica, turning the stems in the hot syrup. Leave for 24 hours, then repeat. Leave for 24 hours and then repeat again.

Drain off the syrup (saving it to use as suggested above). Lay the angelica stems on a rack lined with baking parchment and put into a very low oven (at about 50°C) until dry. This can take anywhere between 2 and 6 hours, depending on the thickness of the stems. The angelica should be dry to the touch, not sticky, but not brittle and desiccated.

Store the candied angelica in an airtight container in a cool, dark cupboard. It will keep for up to 1 year.

# Rosemary and chilli oil

I don't make flavoured oils for long keeping because of the slight risk of botulism. The spores of the bacterium which causes botulism can be present on anything that grows in the earth – including herbs and garlic – and flourish in low-acidity conditions where oxygen is excluded, such as when covered in oil. If you do want to keep flavoured oils, store them in the fridge, where the temperature will inhibit bacterial growth.

Instead, I prefer to make oils like this gorgeous, peppy, fragrant one to be used straight away. It's delicious trickled on pizza or pasta, or over salads, and is the sort of magic ingredient that can turn a motley collection of leftovers (cold rice or potatoes, a few tomatoes, white beans and a scrap of Parmesan, say) into a lovely lunch or supper. You'll have enough here for 6 pasta or pizza servings.

*Makes 150ml*

**1 large stem of rosemary, leaves only, roughly chopped**
**A good pinch of dried chilli flakes**
**1 garlic clove, peeled and cut into slivers (optional)**
**150ml extra virgin olive oil**

Put all the ingredients into a small saucepan and heat gently, so the oil is just fizzing, for 3–5 minutes. Set aside until completely cool, then it is ready to use. You can strain out the flavourings, or not, as you please.

Keep any leftover oil in the fridge and use within a week. If it thickens and turns cloudy, just return to room temperature before using.

# Sweet raspberry vinegar
## with scented geranium

This is based on Pam Corbin's wonderful raspberry vinegar in her *River Cottage Preserves Handbook* (see Directory, p.249). The scented geranium adds another flavour dimension, making this a great addition to a vinaigrette.

*Makes about 750ml*
**500g raspberries**
**4–6 scented geranium leaves**
**300ml white wine vinegar**
**About 225g granulated sugar**

Put the raspberries into a bowl or large jug, along with the scented geranium leaves. Crush them together with the end of a rolling pin, or similar implement. Pour over the wine vinegar. Cover and leave the mixture in the fridge for 4 days, stirring every now and then.

Tip the raspberry mixture into a jelly bag suspended over a large bowl and leave to drip through overnight.

Measure the strained liquid and pour into a saucepan. Add 225g sugar for every 300ml liquid. Heat slowly, stirring, until the sugar has dissolved, then bring to the boil. Boil for about 8 minutes, skimming off any scum, then leave to cool. Bottle and seal when cold. Use within 12 months.

# Rose elixir

This sweet, scented cordial is particularly special – a sort of homemade version of rose water without the overpowering perfumeyness. It's lovely added to drinks, alcoholic or otherwise. For a virgin cocktail, mix 1 part rose elixir to 4 parts chilled apple or pear juice. Serve with ice and a fresh rose petal garnish, or borage flower ice cubes (see p.54). The elixir can also be trickled on to fruit for an exotic salad.

*Makes about 850ml*

50g very fragrant rose petals (around 8 blooms)

Juice of 1 lemon
350g caster or granulated sugar

Put the rose petals into a deep bowl. Pour on 500ml just-boiled water and leave for about 8 hours to infuse. Strain into a pan, crushing out every drop of liquid with a spoon. Add the lemon juice and sugar. Heat gently, stirring, until the sugar has dissolved. Continue to heat until the liquid is steaming hot but not boiling. Pour immediately into warmed sterilised bottles (small ones, as the cordial won't keep well once opened), leaving a 1cm gap at the top, and seal tightly. Cool then store in a cool, dark place for up to 6 months. Once opened, use within a week or two.

# Scented lemonade

This is a really refreshing drink for a hot summer's day. It looks lovely with borage flower ice cubes bobbing in it (see p.54). For a subtly different fragrance, replace the scented geranium leaves with a well-bashed stem of lemongrass.

*Makes about 1.5 litres*

5 lemons
About 8 large (10–15 small) lemon-scented geranium leaves, roughly twisted or crushed
75g caster sugar

Use a potato peeler or sharp knife to pare the zest in thick strips from one of the lemons. Put into a large container with the scented geranium leaves and sugar. Pour on 1.5 litres just-boiled water. Stir to help the sugar dissolve, then leave until completely cool. Squeeze the juice from the lemons and add to the infused liquid. Strain the whole lot into a clean jug and chill before serving, with ice.

# Minty apple mojito

I love a mojito, and with mint straight from the garden and some (inauthentic, but very nice) cloudy fresh apple juice, it's wonderfully refreshing. You can use the traditional soda water in place of the apple juice for a drier drink.

*Per person*

12 fresh spearmint leaves, plus
    extra to garnish
1 tsp caster sugar
Juice of 1 lime (a wedge of the
    squeezed lime reserved)

Crushed ice
50ml white rum
Chilled cloudy apple juice
Lime wedge, to serve

Put the mint, sugar, lime juice and squeezed lime wedge in a tall glass and 'muddle' or crush them together with the end of a wooden spoon or similar implement (a cocktail 'muddler' if you have one). Fill the glass with crushed ice, add the rum, then fill up with apple juice and stir. Finish with a sprig of mint and a lime wedge.

# Sorrel wine cup

A very good use for rather overgrown, mature sorrel leaves, this is based on an old Constance Spry recipe. The sorrel infuses the drink with a subtle lemony acidity.

*Serves 6*

50g bunch of sorrel
3 tsp caster sugar
375ml sweet white wine, such
    as an inexpensive dessert wine

375ml fizzy water
Juice of 2 oranges
Borage flowers, to serve
    (optional)

Tear the sorrel leaves, stalks and all, and put in a plastic container or a jug that will fit in your fridge. Add the sugar and 'muddle' with the sorrel (i.e. crush together with the end of a wooden spoon or similar implement). Add the wine, water and orange juice and stir until the sugar has dissolved. Cover and refrigerate for about 6 hours. To serve, strain into a chilled jug and float a few borage flowers on top.

## Variation
Use 50g salad burnet leaves or sweet cicely, roughly chopped, in place of the sorrel.

# Herb teas

A cup of strongly minty tea, perhaps with just a pinch of sugar, is one of the most refreshing and reviving of drinks. Fantastic as a *digestif* after a meal, lovely as an afternoon cuppa, ideal at any time really if, like me, you sometimes find yourself relying a little too much on the great god caffeine. The mintiness seems to give a little buzz all of its own.

The trick is to be generous. Don't bother making mint tea with less than 3 large sprigs per cup, at least 10 if you're making a pot. Opinions vary as to the best types of mint for tea. Peppermints are more freshly, pungently minty; spearmints are sweeter (see p.105). On balance, I think I'm probably a spearmint girl, but I know others who swear peppermint is the only type for infusions.

Much as I enjoy a pure mint tea, I often use mint as the base, and then season it with a sprig or two of something more penetrating. As I write this, a steaming cup of mint, lemon thyme and lavender tea sits beside me. Lavender is wonderfully soothing in teas. You could also augment mint tea with a leaf or two of sage or lemon verbena, a sprig of lemon balm or the tip of a rosemary stem.

To make a herb tea (technically a tisane), all you need do is pluck your chosen herbs, wash them and check for insect life, then place in a pot or mug. Bring some freshly drawn water to the boil, then let it cool for about 1 minute before pouring on to the herbs, making sure they are completely covered. Water that is absolutely boiling can scald the herbs and damage the flavour. Leave to infuse for at least 5 minutes, or until cool enough to drink. I often like to add a pinch of sugar to enhance a herb tea, but that's purely a matter of taste.

You can also make a very delicious drink by combining garden herbs with standard black tea. I frequently add a generous sprig of lemon balm or bergamot to a brewing mug of afternoon tea. And I add milk too, although drinking it plain black or with a spritz of lemon would also be lovely.

Useful Things

# Directory

## Plants and seeds

You can buy herb seeds or plants at any garden centre, but specialists will always offer you a far greater range, and usually better advice and information too.

### Arne Herbs
www.arneherbs.co.uk
01275 333399
Bristol-based herb specialist.

### Downderry Nursery
www.downderry-nursery.co.uk
01732 810081
Specialist in lavender and rosemary situated in Kent, offering a range of varieties by mail (including *lavandula* x *intermedia* 'Provence'). Website provides good info on planting and nurturing.

### Edulis
www.edulis.co.uk
01635 578113
Berkshire-based grower of rare plants, including unusual herb varieties.

### Green Garden Herbs
www.greengardenherbs.co.uk
01728 452597
Herb specialist based in Aldeburgh, Suffolk. Range includes many lavenders, sages, mints and basils.

### Halsall's Herbs
01206 323158
Herb specialist based in Dedham, Suffolk. Sells herbs at farmers' markets and fairs, and by appointment.

### Jekka's Herb Farm
www.jekkasherbfarm.com
01454 418878
Supplier of a huge range of organic herb plants and seeds by mail order.

### Laurel Farm Herbs
www.laurelfarmherbs.co.uk
01728 668223
Suffolk-based supplier of herb plants by mail order.

### Norfolk Lavender
www.norfolk-lavender.co.uk
01485 570384
Offers a large range of lavender plants by mail (including *lavandula* x *intermedia* 'Provence').

### Otter Farm
www.otterfarm.co.uk
Devon-based organic farm run by Mark Diacono. Shop sells herb plants and seeds (free delivery on seed-only orders).

### Roses UK
www.rosesuk.com
01243 389532
Website listing rose suppliers in the UK. Also gives useful information on many rose varieties.

### Scented Geraniums
www.scentedgeraniums.co.uk
Specialist selling huge range of scented geraniums by mail order, also bags of loose leaves for immediate use. Good advice, growing tips and information too.

## Suffolk Herbs

www.suffolkherbs.com
01376 572456
Supplier of extensive range of herb seeds, including many basils and mints.

## Gardening equipment/supplies

### Harrod Horticultural

www.harrodhorticultural.com
0845 402 5300
Supplier of gardening products, including organic feeds. Also organic herb seeds.

### The Organic Gardening Catalogue

www.organiccatalogue.com
01932 253666
Range of supplies includes herb seeds, organic potting compost and soil improver, organic fertilisers and feeds.

## Websites

### The Herb Society

www.herbsociety.org.uk
0845 491 8699
Fantastic charity working to increase the understanding and use of herbs.

### Garden Organic

www.gardenorganic.org.uk
024 7630 3517
National charity for organic growing, an encyclopedic source of information.

### Recycle Now

www.recyclenow.com
Includes advice on home composting.

## Books

*The Complete Gardener,* Monty Don
Some very good sections on the more commonly used herbs.

*The Great Vegetable Plot,* Sarah Raven
Excellent advice on growing many herbs.

*Growing Herbs,* Jessica Houdret
Herb Society booklet, summarising the basics for many popular herbs.

*Herb and Spice,* Jill Norman
Sound information on the culinary uses of herbs and spices, plus a recipe section.

*Jekka's Complete Herb Book,*
Jekka McVicar
Comprehensive advice on growing herbs.

*McGee on Food and Cooking,*
Harold McGee
Accessible work of kitchen science with a very good section on herbs and spices.

*The River Cottage Hedgerow Handbook,* John Wright
An in-depth look at gathering wild foods.

*The River Cottage Preserves Handbook,* Pam Corbin
Excellent guide to home preserving.

*The River Cottage Veg Patch Handbook,* Mark Diacono
Great advice on establishing your own thriving organic kitchen garden.

# Acknowledgements

There are many people who have generously given their time and shared their wisdom with me during the writing of this handbook. I owe a huge debt of thanks to one colleague in particular, without whom this would be a lesser book. The incredibly talented Mark Diacono has not only brought my words to life with his fantastic photographs but, in his capacity as River Cottage head gardener and general horticultural oracle, has given advice and suggestions that have never failed to help and inspire me. Thank you so much, Mark.

Another fellow author and friend, Pam Corbin, has been as always so generous in sharing her knowledge and experience with me, not to mention a good quantity of her own homegrown herbs.

I must also thank Cheryl Waller of the National Herb Society, whose garden at Sulgrave Manor so inspired me. Also Andrea Halsall of Halsall's Herbs in Dedham, who has provided me with so many thriving herb plants and so much good advice. Andy Strachan, of Garden Organic, has shared some crucial insider info with me, and Peter Miller of King's Seeds (Suffolk Herbs) gave me some excellent information and some very good seeds early on.

Mat Prestwich of R & G Herbs has supplied me with many lush fresh-cut herbs for recipe testing and Trudy Carr at my local farm shop, Brookelynne at Beaumont-cum-Moze, has done the same. Thanks also to the lovely Wendy Sarton of The Fountain House restaurant in Dedham, for loading me up with angelica and good thoughts.

At Bloomsbury, I must thank my charming and enthusiastic editors Natalie Hunt and Richard Atkinson, my wonderful project editor Janet Illsley, and my talented and preternaturally youthful designer Will Webb.

My thanks as always to the River Cottage team, who make it possible for me to do a job I really love – particularly Rob Love and Hugh Fearnley-Whittingstall for giving me the chance to write this book in the first place, and Gill Meller and Oliver Gladwin who did such terrific work cooking for some of the photos.

My deepest love and thanks go to my gorgeous daughters, Tara and Edie, for their love and their faith in me. And last, but really most, I want to thank my parents – the finest anyone could wish for. They've helped with everything from photo shoots to recipe testing (not to mention childcare), and they support and encourage me every day in everything I do. Thanks, Mum and Dad.

# Recipe index

# Index

# River Cottage Handbooks

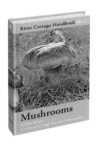

## Seasonal, Local, Organic, Wild

FOR FURTHER INFORMATION AND
TO ORDER ONLINE, VISIT
RIVERCOTTAGE.NET

Whitefield